GW01179594

MEHRDAD YAZDANI

Introduction by Joseph Giovannini

BALCONY PRESS

LOS ANGELES

Copyright © 2005 By Balcony Press.
All Rights Reserved. No part of this book may be reproduced in any manner without written permission of the copyright owners. Every effort has been made to ensure that credits comply with information supplied.

First published in the United States of America by
Balcony Press, an imprint of Balcony Media, Inc.
512 East Wilson, Suite 213
Glendale, California 91206
www.balconypress.com

ISBN 1-890449-29-6

Library of Congress Control Number: 2004110475

Printed in South Korea

Design by John Tom
Edited by Ann Gray and Jesse Brink
Editorial Assistance by Lesley Grant, Alexandra Schioldager, and Cynthia Hilliers

Cover Design and Sketches by Mehrdad Yazdani
Front Cover Photography by Jeff Goldberg
Back Cover Photography by Farshid Assassi

Production by Navigator Cross-media, Los Angeles

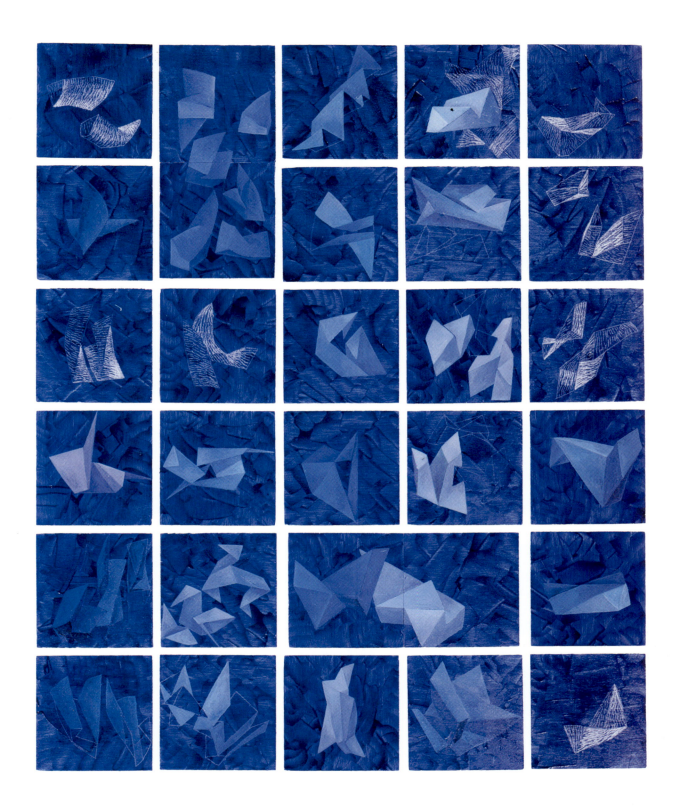

Untitled, 1996
acrylic on wood, 24"x48"
Museum of Modern Art, New York

CONTENTS

006
Introduction
by Joseph Giovannini

016 - 130
Project Essays
by Andrew Blum

Program Complexity

016
Department of Water and Power
Central Distribution Headquarters

024
El Sereno Pool and Recreation Center

028
Kabbalah Children's Academy

032
Sinai Temple Akiba Academy Expansion

036
Hauptman-Woodward Medical
Research Institute

044
Motorcycle Hall of Fame Museum

Sensitivity to Context

048
Centralized Dining and
Student Services Facility,
University of California, Berkeley

054
Glendale Police Headquarters

058
Clark County Detention Center

062
Santa Monica Public Safety Facility

070
Yeshiva University of Los Angeles
Boys High School

076
Oxnard House

080
Tomihiro Museum of Shi-Ga
Competition

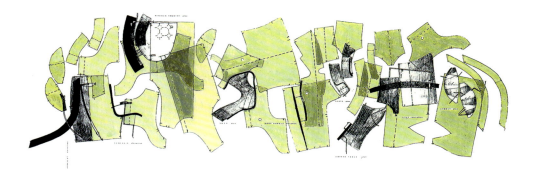 

Integration of Sketches

086
Showscan CineMania Theater

090
Royal Theater Playhouse Competition

094
Queensland Gallery of Modern Art Competition

098
Overland House

Public Engagement

102
Lloyd D. George United States Federal Courthouse

112
Beverly Hills Public Works Building and Water Treatment Facility

118
Los Angeles Metro Red Line Station, Vermont Avenue/Santa Monica Boulevard

126
Duxton Plain Public Housing Competition

130
Guangzhou TV and Sightseeing Tower Competition

132
Selected Projects
1988 - 2005

138
Design Recognition

140
Acknowledgments

141
Credits

INTRODUCTION

Joseph Giovannini

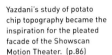

Yazdani's study of potato chip topography became the inspiration for the pleated facade of the Showscan Motion Theater. (p.86)

Mehrdad Yazdani—mild-mannered, soft-spoken, quietly-dressed— does not look particularly subversive, but immediately after graduation from Harvard's School of Design, he acted on what was then an unusual insight: that it was possible for an exponent of avant-garde architecture to infiltrate the business world, and design unexpected, even eccentric work at large scale. Since 1987, he has imported into corporate practice a rarefied design sensibility that seldom escapes from boutique firms. For most of his design career, the Iranian-born, Texas-educated architect has practiced at the intersection of the large office and the small one, producing plans for corporate and institutional clients whose design expectations have seldom been challenged. Not in its wildest board meetings, for example, did the Los Angeles Department of Water and Power think in the mid-1980s that it would need or want air-foil canopies on its facades, diaphanous graphics, corrugated metal siding or rusticated masonry. DWP, nonetheless, was pleased when the architectural awards rolled in. A company founded to serve the public interest was recognized for promoting civic architecture.

All corporate architectural firms proselytize "good design," but Yazdani brings to practice at Cannon Design, where he heads the Yazdani Studio, a particular vision. He has cultivated this vision over years in sketch books that constitute a visual diary. Of all the drawings in the twenty logs that he keeps like references in his office, some 80 percent are independent of any project—ruminations about space, form, color and light. The drawings amount to an imaginative search into issues germane to architecture, yet outside the demands of any specific commission. Influenced, he says, "by things I read and see," the sketches range from moonscapes to sponge studies to omnidirectional labyrinths, and they are reiterative: he revisits themes, developing ideas in progressions of refinement and complexity that, in turn, feed back on themselves in further self-transformation. A long series on the topography of the potato chip metamorphosed into folding planes and then into paintings, before becoming, eventually, the source for the facade of Showscan Show Motion Theater at City Walk at Universal, which featured a pleated, fanning facade animated by electronic imagery. A different iteration of the same idea became the sinuously warped roofscape for the Cesar Chavez/Soto Street Metro Red Line Station in Los Angeles.

For Yazdani, the notebooks have been liberative, a vehicle for pure investigations of architectural conditions that have allowed him to expand his thinking into the physics of space and form.

When Yazdani speculates in his sketchbooks, he is not usually solving a problem: he imagines. Free of program requirements and budget limitations, the drawings are not organizational or propositional but imagistic and spatial, and in their lack of precision, in their conjectural fuzziness, they achieve an oneiric state that permits and even encourages improbability and strangeness. His highly evocative forms and spaces, often drawn in indeterminate colors and irregular geometries, tend to the surreal: the drawing amounts to a way of seeing that mystifies the problem before it can be reduced to a solution. These sketches—in pencil, magic marker, ink and, surprisingly, matter-of-fact ball-point—are the cradles of his work, and they seem very private, as though done unobserved, with little consideration for the boardroom.

It is on these pages that he generates the DNA that filters indirectly into the design process. Walls bend in quizzical deformations that tease perspectival space out of normativeness. Forms may languish in his notebooks for years, or they may be used immediately. The images, in any event, are not flat, graphic and expedient, done in the cursive hand of an architect looking for an efficient answer, but images volumetric, emotive and worked. He turns them in his mind and on the page because they are not the same on all sides: you can't know from one view what the others look like.

The sketchbooks are Yazdani's site of invention, and eventually he applies this research in real commissions, transferring purely spatial and architectural qualities developed on the abstract space of the white page to the exigencies of the project.

Sketches and 3D rendering illustrate the rotating floorplans in the design concept for Mary's Guest House.

Because in these drawings he visualizes building forms three dimensionally, not just in plan, Yazdani develops the vertical dimension, the Z of design, from the first sketches: this is architecture as people will see and experience it. Parts are not simply the resultant forms extruded up from a plan.

In many of his drawings, for example, he investigates turning forms, and eventually the idea has worked its way into actual designs. In drawings for "Mary's Guest House," conceived for an Austin site, he shifts the second floor off the first, and warps a tall vertical wall to meet a roof shifted out of line with the second floor. By the top of the Z axis, then, the floors and roof are no longer coincident: the house has rotated and generated a sense of turning, transforming space.

As applied research, Yazdani's formal enquiries expand the design potential of his buildings, but if the exploration stopped at notions derived from the sketchbooks, the buildings would be limited conceptually by formalism. The drawings, however, are simply an initial step in a design process by which Yazdani enriches buildings beyond the logic of form.

The DWP project in Downtown Los Angeles was seminal for Yazdani because, unlike many Modernists, he was willing to admit into the design many factors and forces emanating from the site. The logic of the design was external as well as internal. At a time when the paradigm of Modernist simplicity had been challenged by Post-Modernist interest in context, Yazdani dislocated the purities of Modernist abstraction by localizing his designs in the specifics of place. He eschewed the universal in favor of the specific. The experience of his buildings tends to intensity because the conditions are unique rather than general.

Yazdani's design methodology for achieving specificity is a process of layering: Yazdani adds. And he adds in a process of reaction. Because the architect does not believe in unitary wholes, in inviolate Platonic solids locked in a gestalt of regularity, he shapes an architecture of parts that remains receptive to change in an open-ended, highly malleable design process. The complexity that results is neither gratuitous nor decorative but instrumental for Yazdani's goal of creating a building that is experientially generous and enduring. He designs buildings that change in perception and fact: as in a painting that continues to intrigue the eye of the viewer because of a complex skein of relationships understood over time, Yazdani's buildings yield in their layering a multiplicity of readings.

Yazdani enriches his designs through a collagist technique and combinatory sensibility. As a three-dimensional collagist, Yazdani layers forms omnidirectionally. The results are spaces of change, one form reading past the next in a sequence of heightened difference. Yazdani came of age aesthetically during the 1980s, as architecture schools were emerging from the blandishments of Post Modernist historicity. He did not, however, resort to the obvious fall-back position of a retro-Modernism, but pursued instead a philosophical calling that emphasizes difference over sameness, diversity over unity. His Modernism did not assume the totalizing logic of industrial production, in which parts are serially produced in repetitive sameness. He rejected the homogenizing aesthetic of mass industrial production. The artistic content of his notebooks afforded Yazdani grounds for conceptual resistance to the juggernaut of repetitive sameness that industrialized construction has traditionally encouraged—at least before the arrival of the computer on the construction site. Today, as manufacturers realize that one size no longer fits all, builders are opening to notions of computer-assisted complexity and variety. Machines with chips that think can produce differentiated components that have a role in the kind of architecture Yazdani designs.

Study models for the Royal Theater Playhouse competition illustrate the two reciprocal wedges comprising the building mass. (p. 90)

When Yazdani imported a more singular vision into corporate practice, then, he was saying that the vision was not precious and applicable only within the realm of privileged boutique commissions. If the ideas are valid, they should be robust enough to survive and even thrive in the corporate and bureaucratic worlds. Yazdani did not want to design down.

The success of his insight, however, was not a self-evident eventuality, but one that required Darwinian adaptation. His budgets have been limited rather than generous, and many of the jobs in the public realm have required lowest construction bids. Without a contractor on board because of the competitive bidding process, Yazdani could not risk designs dependent on unattainable details. The architect adjusted his design away from the precious detail in favor of broad strokes. Yazdani had to choose his materials judiciously and even defensively, allowing wide tolerances for craft. A vision rooted in delicate, even fragile drawings had to face the reality of constructibility in demanding building environments. In Yazdani's practice, then, God has migrated from the detail to the gesture, to larger moves and their impact of the building perceived at a distance in a sympathetic relationship to its context. Close up the richness is material: he cultivates texture, integral color and tactility.

Although it is not a standard practice of Cannon Design, the firm at which Yazdani is a principal and lead designer, to accept house commissions, Yazdani's talent has been to infuse large- and medium-scale projects with the intensity more usually seen in small-scale work. The scheme he proposed in a competition for The Royal Theater Playhouse in Copenhagen, for example, shows two reciprocal wedges, each slightly deformed, open to each other and the waterside site: one dips down, as though touching the water with its forward point. Such designs are not only provocative but evocative, and Yazdani has proposed for the public realm a civic mystery that seems as natural here as it would be in the leafier, more private realms of suburbia. The city has no less need for enigma and artistic intensity than the private sphere. Yazdani opens the collective psyche to spatial delights that characteristically have been the province of more cloistered worlds. Yazdani practices at the nexus of fantasy and practicality. Each is tensed by the presence of the other; each is richer for the tension.

As an architect of complexity, or at least apparent complexity, Yazdani differentiates each of the components of the program in one or several ways—form, material, color, light—and juxtaposes the parts so that they read visually in contradistinction to each other. In the El Sereno Pool and Recreation Center, for instance, a commission that initially threatened to become yet another mindless instance of Spanoid Colonial, he collages corrugated metal, stucco, cyclone fencing, steel and glazed brick into a material composition that reinforces the idea of an athletic roof springing over the static, earthbound elements of the program. In the more recent Public Works building, for the City of Beverly Hills, and the Hauptman-Woodward Institute Research Headquarters in Buffalo, he makes extensive use of u-channel glass in juxtaposition to plaster and metal, to produce a collagistic composition with a luminosity that emits a strong ethereal effect.

In an age of gypsum board, when many new buildings lack the feeling of substance, Yazdani cultivates the tactile through a choice of materials which substantiate each of his successive architectural layers. Changing materials in close proximity to each other heightens the differentiation of the parts and their spatial separation. Yazdani also uses color to differentiate spaces and surfaces, especially when breaking down a mass. He prefers to use colors that are integral to a material rather than applied—"more sincere," he says.

Yazdani layers texture and color to manipulate natural light within his spaces, as with the Beckman Business and Technology Hall at Chapman University.

In a variation of his layering technique, he compounds sensations. The architect coats the stairwell in the Beckman Business & Technology Hall at Chapman University in Santa Ana, California, in a polished Venetian plaster, and he ignites the colors by orchestrating sunlight so that it falls through the skylight, glancing on its surfaces. Yazdani uses the sun as an element to give an additional dimension to a space that forms the heart of the structure. The plaster, reciprocally, colors the light. He adds each to the other in a contained room, as though mixing the two in a spatial bucket. Yazdani may normally start with a neutral palette of silvers, off-whites or grays, but at special moments, he chooses a strong, punctual color and then heightens the effect with light so that it becomes phenomenal. He enriches his designs through phenomenological enticements: he conceives buildings so they invite the environment to reflect on buildings in changing ways. The heightened coloration and luminosity marks the space as the heart of the building, and attracts students away from the elevators into what becomes the building's socializing centerpiece.

Sometimes the most tangible material comes laden with immaterial associations, such as memory and history. At the Yeshiva University Boys High School in Los Angeles, Yazdani uses Jerusalem stone, which taps into collective memory because of its connotations of its Middle Eastern history. Yazdani himself hails from a culture over 2,500 years old, and because Iran has always evolved by building on its past, Yazdani is predisposed culturally to respect clients interested in the existing site and the culture and history of the institution. As a Modernist, however, and as an adult who has spent more of his life in America than in Iran, he does not react with literalism: he does not imitate history.

Yazdani cultivates memory through abstraction. His clients at Contra Costa County Public Safety Command Center, within an existing complex dominated by buildings with Spanish tile roofs, expected a reiteration of this shop-worn architectural mantra. But Yazdani instead floated an undulating red roof over a strictly geometric plinth of a building, tying the roofs together in a dialogue of difference rather than identity. The strategy respects the past while introducing a new future. Operating from two cultural backgrounds, Yazdani looks both backward and forward in time.

For Yazdani light itself is an element to be deployed like a constituent brick in the construction of a building, and his sketchbooks document a long interest in developing light as a material. In the case of the Yeshiva high school, the golden Jerusalem stone glows with the intensity of the Southern California sun, and the sharp chiaroscuro effects recall the raking Mediterranean light of the Levant. In many interiors he designs artificial light with comparably subtle effect, couching light in the interstices of building parts articulated by their separation: the lights are never seen head on, but glow, revealed by the matter they illuminate.

In his drawings, Yazdani sculpts light so that it reveals form. He studies light entering space through windows and side walls; he hypothesizes light entering from above, and light reflecting off surfaces. All the while, the studies tap into the memory of places he has seen. In the sketchbooks he recreates the experience abstractly. There is no hint of historicity or sentimentality, simply light as element.

The larger idea behind Yazdani's interest in the sun and the effects he can cultivate on a building is the phenomenological potential of architecture—ephemeral effects that change with the hour, the season and the weather. He believes that the sun is a device capable of changing the experience of a building, whether on its surfaces or as it finds its way inside, playing off forms and spaces. For Yazdani, light can reveal dimension, proportion and quality; it is integral to the experience of a space. The experience, however, can be multiple and simultaneous. In one sketchbook, he draws a curved wall that receives

Sketchbook drawings investigate the effects of light traveling through varying spaces.

light in a continuous gradient of shadow, and adds a flat sun screen to the surface, on which the light looks angular, even folded. When he designed the facade of the Clark County Detention Center in Las Vegas, with its narrow window slots, he animated the facade of cells by placing butterfly shades, made in perforated metal, over the windows, which relieve their monotony with the flutter of glancing light and deep shadow. The play forms a permanently impermanent pattern across the facade.

The building may not move, but the sun does, and as architect, he sets up a systematic visual device that acts as an architectural sundial indexing the movement of light and shade. This facade, in association with others in this volumetrically complex composition of blocks, belies the fact that the building is a detention center occupying a large parcel on a prominent block in the center of the city.

The separation of building components into architectural parts that are left discrete rather than homogenized into wholes affords the opportunity of specific luminosity. Yazdani often underscores the distinctions between constituent parts by cracking open the envelope, admitting natural light through the gaps, allowing light to flood in through the reveals between the parts. In the maintenance pen for DWP, used for truck repair, the overhead lights are hardly ever turned on because of the multiple points of entry for natural light through the porous structure. Porosity, of course, has been a recurrent theme throughout his sketchbooks.

Yazdani's commitment to drawing and painting developed during his teenage years in a high school in Tehran specialized in the training of artists and architects. Convinced that he would be an artist, he studied drawing seriously, but his original interest in painting expanded to embrace sculpture. During a sequence of summers, he happened to sit in on his sister's architecture classes, and came to feel that both painting and sculpture, for him, were limiting: he became more interested in architecture, which he felt to be liberating.

Drawing, however, has remained an abiding interest, and it still serves as a vehicle of speculation. "I try to sculpt the drawing with the pen, to spatialize the object," he says. The drawings give him the sensation of vicarious experience: "I've been to those spaces, because I've drawn them." When he visits real buildings with unique spatialities, he often feels he knows them, because the buildings tap into the memory of constructs he has imagined on paper.

Often the drawings start as a question that invites a visual response. One series began when Yazdani saw an ad of a samurai wrestler sitting on a chair; the wrestler's bulk made the chair look tiny. "I started wondering what you can do to a small space that would make the elements look big," he remembers. He started distorting space by tapering walls, compressing the floor and ceiling so that objects in the space bulged out, getting bigger at the top. Perspective reversed. Compressing the volumes monumentalized the forms. "By drawing the idea, I visited the space: it registered in my memory," he says. The image of the samurai space proved salient to the commission for the design of a 2,500-unit public housing competition submission in Singapore, where the architect had to densify a small urban site, while leaving enough space for a park and playgrounds.

The imagistic spillover of the drawings into the buildings often yields a strong iconic presence that enhances the structure's civic profile. The afterimage is not accidental: Yazdani believes that architecture is the most public of the arts, and he uses design to draw the public into a civic engagement with the building through an act of attraction.

Early conceptual sketches for the Contra Costa Sheriff's Comand Center in Martinez, CA are translated to three-dimensional computer drawings.

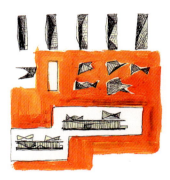 

Iconic imagery is a strong step toward this engagement. In his Metro Red Line Station at Vermont Avenue and Santa Monica Boulevard, done while he was with Ellerbe Becket, Yazdani suspended an elliptically shaped canopy over the entrance that just narrowly escaped the value engineers. The 30-foot-high shape hovers weightlessly and acrobatically over the escalators, a rhetorical device that monumentalizes the corner subway station as it confers a ceremonial quality. At night, the illumination transforms the canopy into a civic lantern, both high-tech and quizzical.

Balanced on edge and buoyant, the curious form is the handle by which people see and understand the station and the invisible metro underground: the mysterious shape has emerged as one of the most admired symbols of the city. Yazdani wanted to design something that would pique the curiosity of passers-by, elevate their awareness, and make them participate within what becomes an interpretative environment. The form is a civic question mark that invites responses.

The icon need not be an object. In the Lloyd D. George United States Courthouse in Las Vegas, it was public space. Judges, as architectural clients, frequently yearn for the archetypal symbol of the American courthouse, the flight of stairs leading up to a portico of columns. Never mind that this image is often considered an authoritarian symbol of oppression by minority groups. Yazdani was able to satisfy the judges while defusing the onerous imagery by creating an impressive flight of stairs up to a vast, seven-story public porch slipping under an open quadrant of the new courthouse. A steel column, tapering top and bottom and bulging in exaggerated entasis in the middle, holds up a roof trellis that the column appears at the same time to tether down.

Yazdani has created a public space that emerges as a civic symbol: the entrance is practical—lawyers make their deals here—yet it is ceremonial: the court holds gatherings in the space, and school groups spontaneously stage group portraits here. Yazdani has orchestrated all the architectural elements that create a civic moment—a monumental space consummating a flight of stairs with a roof supported by a heroic column—without being literal about symbols. A modernist, he transformed traditional symbols and notions of civic grandeur into equivalents that are removed in their abstraction. He re-presents the grandeur in a non-familiar way. The building becomes a focus of the community and part of its memory. People in Las Vegas will identify with the building as they identify the building with the city.

Yazdani adds to the iconic content of his structures, affirming the civic nature of his projects, by cultivating its public life. In Las Vegas, he affirms the urban character of the building with a public promenade. A linear series of outdoor spaces— walled, landscaped and furnished with benches designed by artists—collects people leaving the parking lot and leads them to the civic verandah, where they enter the building under a glazed, seven-story rotunda that allows framed views of the facade above and the building to come. Louvers in the canopy shade the plaza in summer time, striating the pattern dramatically in a zebra pattern of light and shade. This carefully choreographed progression of outdoor spaces continues inside. On the upper floors, spacious 16-foot-tall corridors with glass walls allow views of downtown framed by the column of the verandah. The public circulation reconnects citizens to the city, giving the building's mission of justice a sense of a larger, civic context.

In a water treatment plant component for the Public Works commission in Beverly Hills, Yazdani injected public uses into a building type normally closed to the street and opaque to public understanding. Yazdani designed the entrance lobby so that it doubles as a reception area, and he created an adjacent garden court open to the street, with a water fountain that doubles as an amphitheater when dry, where summer concerts and other outdoor events are staged. Events in the lobby and the court spill into each other. A strong, subtly undulating roof hovers over the composition of solids and voids, unifying

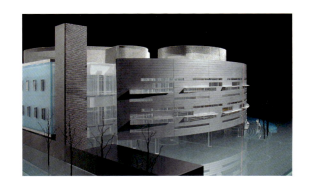

The circlular and square programmatic elements that shape the Hauptman-Woodward Institute are inspired by the coexistence of intuition and reason at the essence of scientific research. (p.36)

the disparate parts. An overhang of the roof, supported by a lithe, metal-sheathed column, forms a three-story portico that marks the entrance to the plant.

The building is not simply handsome: Yazdani has diversified its programmatic content and cultivated functions that extrovert an inherently introverted building type with consequences that enhance the life of the city. He designs not just the forms but also proliferates functions that proactively engage the public. The open forms of the design underscore his tactics for opening the building as an institution to the city. The water treatment facility, normally hermetically sealed in a closed structure, looks like the cultural facility Yazdani has effectively created through a reinterpretation of program. It could be a museum.

Yazdani also cultivates a sense of community within his buildings. In dense, traditional cities, urbanism is a product of street life, but in cities whose infrastructure developed after the advent of the car, buildings must often cultivate inside the urbanism that doesn't exist outside. The desire for the interior life that Yazdani creates in most of his building was all the more acute in the Hauptman-Woodward Institute Research Headquarters in Buffalo, New York, where the clients wanted to demystify science by making visible how scientists work. They also wanted to encourage communication among colleagues.

To invite the dialogue, and to make it visible, Yazdani simply polarized the building, placing the labs in a square, compact block and the scientists' offices in a semi-circular wing that hinges on one side of the block and pivots around a wedge-shaped three-story atrium. Instead of plying stairwells, the scientists shuttle between their labs and offices across the light-filled atrium, frequently encountering one another in informal meetings in a public space that Yazdani cross-programs vertically with a lunch room on a lower floor and a library on an upper floor. Other devices, such as balconies overlooking the atrium help socialize the space further; windows from the offices into the atrium encourage an interactive visual relationship between the office and the atrium. Yazdani creates a vertical piazza.

Yazdani refers to the forces affecting a site as the "energy diagram," and his design for the GTE Middle School in Long Beach, California, absorbs and reflects many considerations outside any internal logic of the commission. The triangular site, for example, drops fifteen feet in elevation from north to south, which prompted the architect to layer the program vertically, stacking classrooms and administration wings. Taking advantage of the changes in topography, he works the geometry of the site vertically, establishing dynamic forms whose diagonal lines force the eye deeply into space, vertically as well as horizontally, in what amounts to sophisticated plays of cross perspective deriving from perspectival studies in his sketchbooks. The floating entrance roof, a Yazdani signature, frames the thrusting view into the main courtyard; a ramp starts at the entrance and heads down to ground that itself slopes. What appear to be single-story buildings on the street reveal themselves to be a two-story complex whose height gives strong definition to the outdoor public spaces. Yazdani organized the classrooms so that they form a large and small courtyard, which create socializing spaces very different from the open yards so characteristic of schools in Southern California: Yazdani introduces an urbanizing spatiality to students who rarely encounter the typology outside the commercialism of malls.

Yazdani aggregated the buildings toward the center of the triangular site, to allow future growth outwards toward the perimeter. His strategy was to energize the center, and build out from that energy. He has factored civic space into the DNA of the present complex and its future extensions.

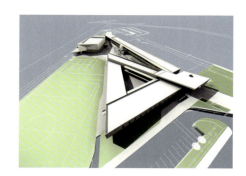

The arrangement and design of buildings for the Long Beach GTE Middle School are responsive to a unique, angular site.

Counterintuitively, the floor plans themselves are relatively simple.

Over a period of time, the vector of an architect's work points to different directions, Yazdani has recently sought greater clarity in the geometry of the forms, and a different kind of complexity. In the Contra Costa County Public Safety Building, Yazdani diagrammed the general layout as a doughnut and organized the three-story building in what he calls a "tabletop," on which he places several building objects: the two-story base of the building serves as an acropolis for what appear to be quasi-independent structures on the third floor, acting visually as pavilions. The red roof, derived from the potato chip studies, floats above the ensemble of forms in a fluid, unifying gesture.

In the Hauptman laboratories in Buffalo, Yazdani reduced the building to a combination of interlocking elemental forms, the square, oval and circle, simplifying complexity with an application of geometrically identifiable volumes. Still, the elemental forms are incomplete, and therefore open, and the circle pivots around the square off-axis, setting the volumes into a visual and spatial dynamic.

The architect draws a permeable line between simplicity and complexity, and then affirms the ambiguity through a material layering of glass: Yazdani sets up a shifting play between flat, reflective surfaces and spatial depth by juxtaposing transparent glass, opaque white spandrel panels and translucent glass channels. Even though individual forms may be simplified, relative to previous work, their syntactic relationship remains spatially complex. Even the reduction of the materials to a palette of glass achieves a simplicity in concept but not appearance: Yazdani's use of glass types may achieve a diaphanous effect, but it is still collage. Yazdani is disciplining the work to the essential moves that he sets in subtle relationships, "to achieve more with less," he says, "not that less is more."

If there are shifts of form and attitude within the portfolio of Yazdani's career, the richness remains a thread linking all the iterations. What characterizes the search in both the sketchbooks and the built structures is a quest within a matrix of richness that Yazdani invents as a matter of both principle and sensibility. The sum total of all the sketchbooks reveals a restless design intelligence pursuing issues that invite the destabilization of questions more than the stasis of answers.

The character of his architectural subjects may slide into different terrains, but their interaction—the dynamic between form, program, materials, light and the public sphere—guarantees that the architecture is complete in its scope of subjects, and alive in their interaction. Yazdani's collagist sensibility is not a formalist end in itself, but reinforces his drive to enhance and intensify designs with successive overlays of meaning and experience. Invariably the richness that he designs into his structures helps build the institutions that they house and the senses and sensibility of their occupants.

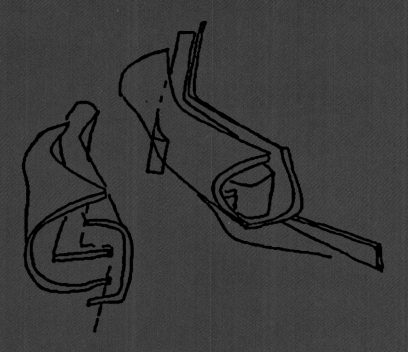

These sometimes distorted, sometimes dynamized forms that take shape within sketchbook pages often mask clear organizational diagrams laid out with a succession of programmed spaces that follow logically from the front door. The plan diagram certainly informs the exterior of the building, but does not dominate. The differentiations visible on the exterior, continue inside, so that interiors emerge as facades distinguished by materials and forms that straddle the inside-outside membrane. Complexity is achieved not through the plan but through the distribution of the program, the variability of the section, and the path of natural light streaming between volumes.

PROGRAM COMPLEXITY

DEPARTMENT OF WATER AND POWER
CENTRAL DISTRIBUTION HEADQUARTERS

Los Angeles, California

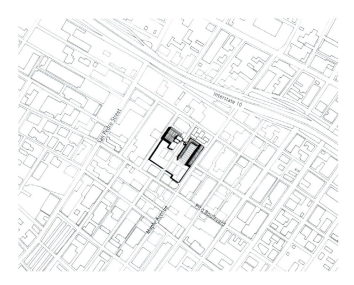

The designs for these buildings for the Department of Water and Power were driven by pressure from the Los Angeles Cultural Affairs Commission for the department to reinvigorate its distinguished architectural tradition of the 1960s. The buildings draw on their industrial setting for their forms and materials, even as they demonstrate an evolution in design sensibility—a stylistic shift from post-modernism to a more refined modernism.

Administration Building and Warehouse

Each of the three programmatic elements in the 55,000-square-foot Administrative Office Building and Warehouse in downtown Los Angeles is identified by a specific volume: a square wing for administrative offices, a rectangular warehouse, and a cylindrical assembly room connecting the two. The two-story office wing is intersected by a concrete-block cylinder crowned by a rectangular glass block. Separating the functions breaks up the mass of the building while also suggesting a machine-like rationality. While the building's traditional architectural elements—framed windows, walls with a clearly articulated bottom, middle and top, and the use of plaster and concrete block—are balanced by shy bits of modernism, such as a glazed corner supported by a single round column, and a subtle abstraction in the composition of the facades.

The rationality behind the building's composition reveals the influence of Russian constructivism, with each function having its own shape and cladding. The glass block crown also echoes the nearby downtown office slabs, while the cylinder mirrors the curved guardhouse of the adjacent Fleet Services Building to form an entrance to the complex. The warehouse section of the building has a distinctive saw-tooth roof that animates the exterior volume and admits natural light, at minimal additional cost. Inside, a two-story entrance hall contains a curving sculptural stair, paved in white terrazzo inlaid with black marble chips—a characteristic detail squeezed into tight program and a tighter budget.

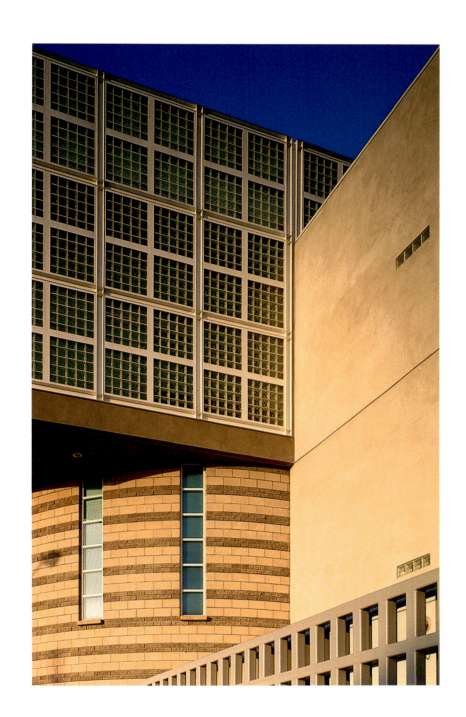

∧ Administration Building detail.

< View to Cafeteria entry.

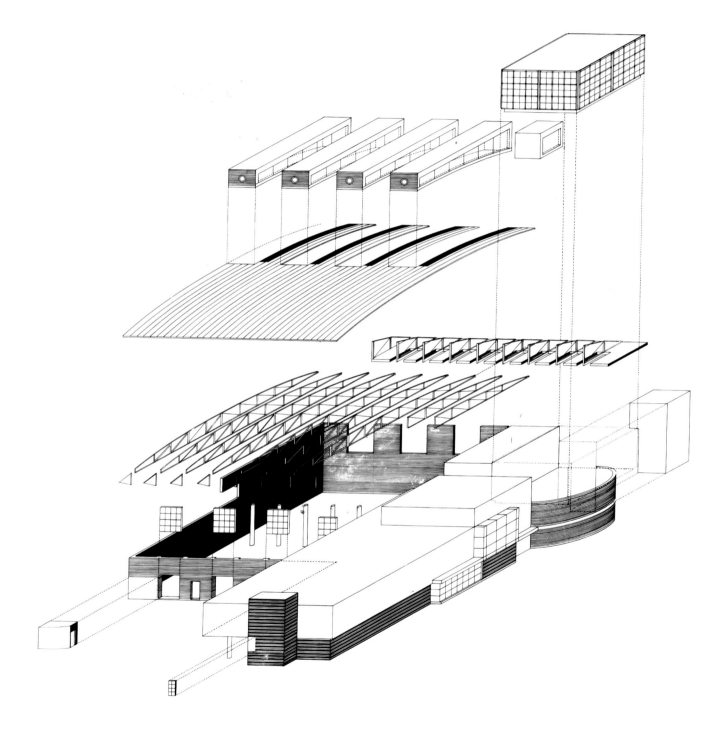

< Exploded axonometric diagram of Administration Building and warehouse.

v Warehouse canopy and skylights.

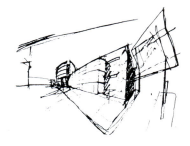
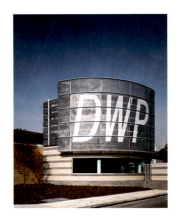
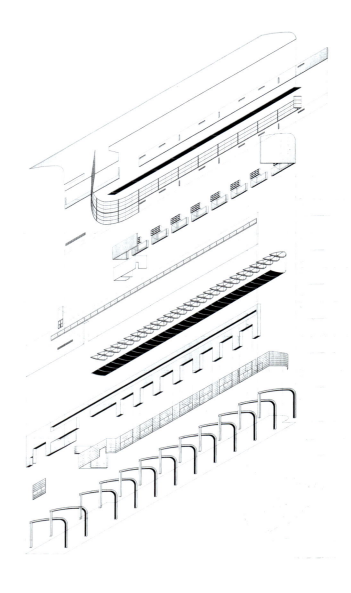

Fleet Services Facility

The L-shaped Fleet Services Building completes the four-acre downtown Los Angeles DWP complex, and demonstrates a formal evolution. While the office building and warehouse are volumetrically composed, the programmatic elements of this service garage and storage shed are distinguished by characteristic wall planes. For example, a continuous plane of translucent fiberglass panels runs through the building: at the front elevation it serves as a sheathing for the protruding doorway, inside it curves to partition a lunch area, and at the rear it emerges outside again as exterior cladding. Its passage becomes a critique of the way buildings (particularly utilitarian ones) are put together, by revealing the complex process of assembling parts into a cohesive whole. Similarly, the spatial envelope of the building was derived from the dimensions of the trucks to be serviced. The guardhouse, which serves the entire complex, is shaded by a curved scrim of perforated steel, which becomes the background for a super-graphic DWP logo. The back wall of the service building is pulled out to the street wall—emphasizing that while this is necessarily a fortress-like complex in a gritty industrial area, it can also be a pleasant place to work, an inexpensive building to maintain, and a formal exploration of the architecture of Los Angeles' infrastructure.

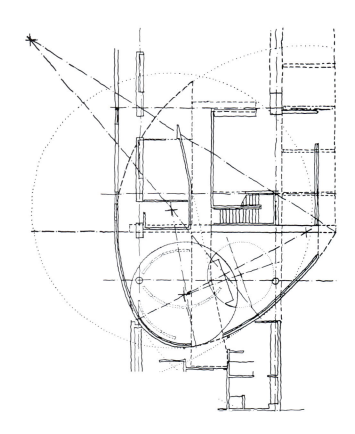

∧ Interior and exterior views of Fleet Services facility.

> Plan diagram.

>> Fleet Services facility entrance and service bays.

>> Building and canopy detail.

EL SERENO POOL AND RECREATION CENTER

Los Angeles, California

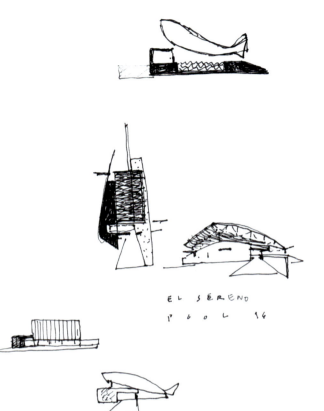

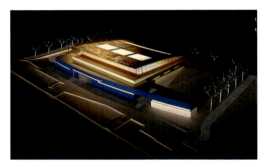

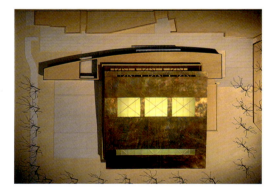

For their new public pool, the tight-knit Los Angeles neighborhood of El Sereno expected a concrete box with a red tile roof—a "Taco Bell on steroids." Instead, they were given a dynamic modern building whose design reflects the contours of the surrounding hills, while being robust enough to stand up to both a limited construction budget and the threat of vandalism.

At El Sereno this meant embracing an industrial aesthetic and details that could survive construction on the cheap—like an internally expressed structure, garage doors, concrete flooring and glass blocks. A gently arched copper roof gives the building a distinctive, energetic, silhouette—like a swimmer reaching through the water—while visually linking it to the surrounding hills. The mullions of the clerestory windows similarly lean, create the impression of a dynamically poised lantern resting on top of a simple concrete base. Additional natural light is filtered through three large skylights, made of translucent fiberglass to minimize potentially dangerous reflections on the water. Roll-up garage doors expose the pool area to summer breezes, while mesh metal screens maintain security and create a layering of materials that lends an unexpected and sophisticated sense of porosity. Support spaces—locker rooms, offices, equipment areas and a classroom—are contained in an adjacent low pavilion clad in blue-glazed tile and glass brick. In plan it arcs towards the property edge, mimicking the sectional arc of the pool while metaphorically reaching out to the community. Raw Corten steel panels surround the entryway, bringing a rich materiality at minimal cost.

The architecture of the El Sereno pool tweaks standard forms while elegantly deploying tough materials. It demonstrates that, even for a Los Angeles Department of Recreation and Parks project with a bare-bones budget, architectural quality need not cost extra.

∧ View to north facade.

> Plan.

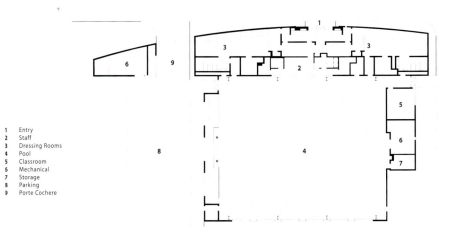

1 Entry
2 Staff
3 Dressing Rooms
4 Pool
5 Classroom
6 Mechanical
7 Storage
8 Parking
9 Porte Cochere

Ground Floor Plan

∧ Interior view, swimming pool facility.

< Northwest corner of complex.

> Entry detail illustrates variety of contrasting materials.

KABBALAH CHILDREN'S ACADEMY

Los Angeles, California

The design of the Kabbalah Children's Academy reflects the interweaving of spiritual and physical reality at the heart of Kabbalistic teaching. The 40,000-square-foot complex packs classrooms, offices, library, gymnasium and support functions into a tight urban site, creating an unexpected campus in the heart of a high-traffic commercial corridor in Los Angeles. The front of the building rises to face the bustle of La Cienega Boulevard, while the rear has a lower profile, allowing for light-filled outdoor spaces.

Its architectural language reflects Kabbalistic notions: it invokes massiveness and softness, security and safety, while manipulating form, space and light to challenge common expectations. Its parti is defined by a series of planes that wind through the building like a ribbon, delimiting spaces while tying them all together—as Kabbalah interweaves the spiritual and the physical. While regulations for educational spaces dictate that children of different age groups cannot share classrooms and certain activity areas, the use of transparent materials and screens creates visual connections, encouraging interaction. The result is a sense of openness, connection and surprise: a bridge leads from a classroom to an outdoor playground; a staircase ascends through curved walls to a rooftop basketball court; and exterior balconies recall a ship's deck, in reference to the academy's philosophy of education as a journey. By creating a space that encourages its own physical exploration, the design reinforces the academy's desire to promote spiritual, educational and imaginative exploration.

Model – building front on La Cienega Boulevard.

Ground Floor - Preschool

Second Floor - Classrooms

Third Floor - Gymnasium

Rooftop Playground

1. Ground floor view to entry from courtyard.
2. Ground floor entry view to courtyard.
3. Courtyard view from ground floor reception.
4. Library/Beit Midrash.
5. View to (rear of building) and courtyard/playground.
6. Courtyard/playground.
7. Play area detail.
8. Third floor gymnasium.
9. View to south end of building, rooftop.

1

2

3

4

5

6

7

8

9

v   Model – southeast view to rear of building.

SINAI TEMPLE AKIBA ACADEMY EXPANSION

Los Angeles, California

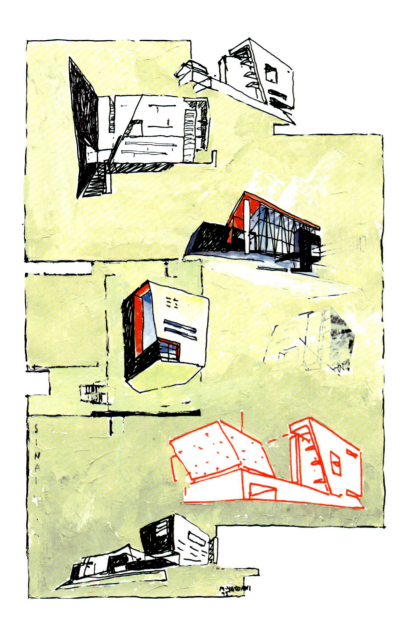

The expansion of the Sinai Temple Akiba Academy required a puzzle-master's approach to context and program. Any addition had to respond to the strong character of the original buildings, designed in the 1950s and 1970s by Frank Lloyd Wright disciple Sidney Eisenstadt, while packing the constricted site with 60,000 square feet of classrooms, a gymnasium, outside play areas, multi-purpose rooms, and underground parking for 350 cars. The context required that the new building accommodate a shift in neighborhood scale and character—one side of the building fronts a busy boulevard while the other faces a quiet residential street.

The design responds with a geometric collage that breaks up both the massing and the fenestration while maintaining a consistency of materials, primarily pre-cast concrete. The pavilion facing Beverly Glen—a wide, busy street—is high and assertive. But its orthogonal mass contains pre-school classrooms and a gym, which is visible from the street behind translucent panels. Beneath a cantilevered corner, an entrance staircase rises between walls of Jerusalem stone. At one edge of the building the façade is pulled away from the stair core, recalling the folded planes of the original temple while creating outdoor space. The rear pavilion, in contrast, is both smaller in scale and more sculpted, with a bowed roof that responds to Eisenstadt's geometries. A two-story glass façade faces a podium-level courtyard, with an enclosed playground for the preschoolers. Parking is accommodated on four underground levels, with additional room for pickup and drop-off queuing.

By emphasizing functional adjacencies both horizontally and vertically, the building creates an urban campus—achieving in a half city block what suburban schools often spread out over several acres.

∧ View to building entry at Beverly Glen Boulevard and Ashton Avenue.

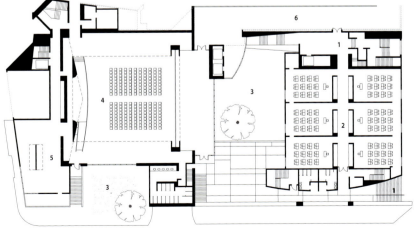

1 Entry
2 Classrooms
3 Courtyard / Playground
4 Multipurpose Room
5 Kitchen
6 Existing Building

Ground Floor Plan

> Southwest view to expansion along Ashton Avenue.

< Courtyard view west to building.

v Gymnasium interior.

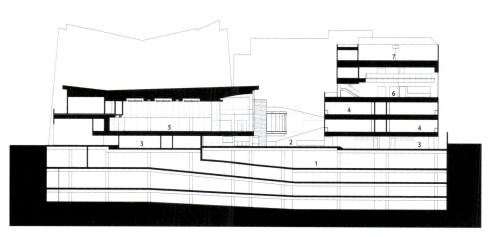

1 Parking
2 Courtyard / Playground
3 Preschool Classrooms
4 Elementary Classrooms
5 Multipurpose Room
6 Indoor Gym
7 Rooftop Play Area

Section

HAUPTMAN-WOODWARD MEDICAL RESEARCH INSTITUTE

Buffalo, New York

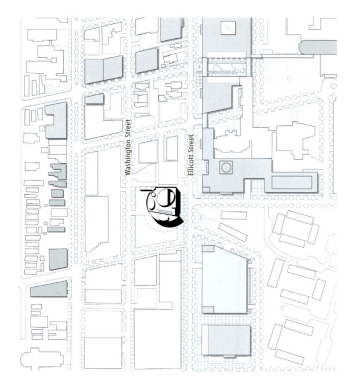

Scientific research institutions increasingly recognize architecture as an important feature in attracting talent and creating a setting that inspires the creativity necessary for scientific advancement. For their new structural biology research facility, the Hauptman-Woodward Institute in Buffalo demanded a building of world class caliber—not an idle term for an institution led by a Nobel Laureate. As a gateway to the Buffalo Niagara Medical Campus, the 70,000-square-foot building sought to take its place alongside the landmarks of Buffalo's past, but with a twenty-first century spirit of design integrity and scientific purpose.

The program shaped the design into a three-part geometry: a rectilinear translucent laboratory wing, a curved office wing and a three-story atrium joining the two. The combination of the purity of the square and the fluidity of the curve reflects the dynamic coexistence of intuition and reason at the heart of scientific research: the curved office section symbolically houses the scientific mind while a square lab section holds the tools.

Laboratory buildings have traditionally placed researchers' offices adjacent to their individual labs, but here the offices have been consolidated in an architecturally distinct section of the building, joined to the laboratory block by the atrium. The 'vertical piazza' that results encourages interaction and serves as the building's social hub. In the evening, the atrium glows like a lantern, serving as a beacon to define the institute's entry, projecting the activity within to the streetscape, and symbolizing its spirit of innovation. The laboratory block—which is rectilinear for greatest efficiency—is similarly enclosed with semi-transparent u-channel glass that from the street silhouettes the scientists working within and seeks to demystify their activities to the public. The curve of the office block provides a more private, contemplative setting for the scientists. The offset windows bring a sense of individuality to the offices, while sunscreens above block the summer sun, reducing demand for air-conditioning and artificial illumination.

∧ Building entry along Ellicott Street.

> View to curved facade of the building's south end.

\> Northwest view to building along Ellicott Street.

v Four views of curved window wall.

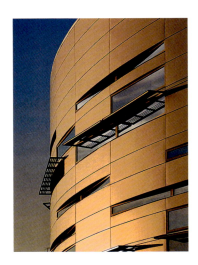   

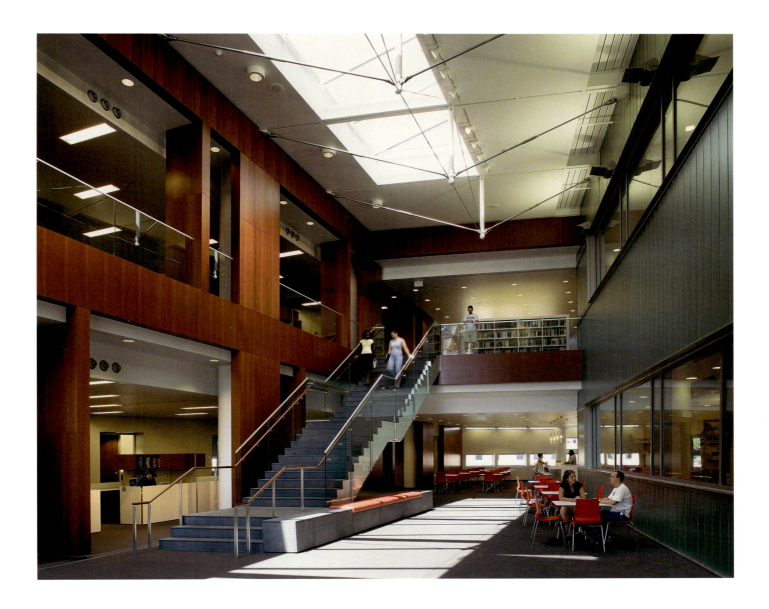

∧ Second floor cafe and common areas, and with view to offices and third floor library.

< View of laboratory wall and ground floor entry from stair.

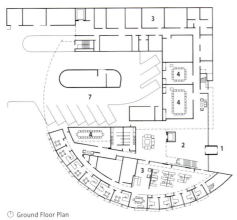

Ground Floor Plan

Second Floor Plan

1 Entry
2 Atrium
3 Offices
4 Seminar / Lecture
5 Laboratories
6 Lunch / Lounge Area
7 Parking / Loading

> Detail of laboratory work space.

>> Laboratory view from atrium.

v Northeast window wall detail.

MOTORCYCLE HALL OF FAME MUSEUM

Columbus, Ohio

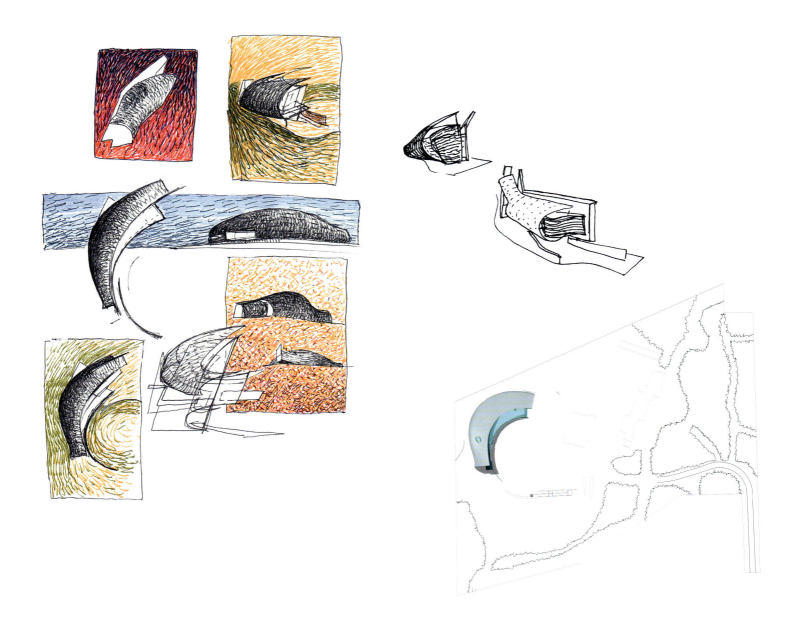

The design for the American Motorcyle Association's Motorcycle Hall of Fame seeks to connect the sensations of the open highway with the museum experience. Located on a site clearly visible from Interstate 70, outside Columbus, Ohio, the 60,000-square-foot building is conceived as its own billboard, with a sculptural façade that recalls a motorcycle fender. When seen at highway speeds, its form appears to shift and shimmer, drawing visitors with the promise of a museum experience befitting the sensory excitement of motorcycling itself.

The curve of the building wraps around a wheel-shaped entry court for pedestrian drop-off and motorcycle parking. Corten steel cladding lends the front façade a machine-like character, while remaining sympathetic to the existing wood-sided buildings on the site, which was originally the headquarters of an insurance company. Sandblasted super-graphics subtly spell out the museum's function.

Inside the museum, exhibits are placed along a ramp that spirals up, drawing visitors through the galleries and emphasizing the sensation of movement through space. The exhibits themselves—meant to celebrate the heroes of motorcycling, rather than their machines—are arranged as singular events to be experienced over the course of the longer journey up the ramp. The curved rear wall of the exhibition area has exposed structural ribs that emphasize the industrial, almost garage-like, character of the space. A café, museum shop and boardroom are located in a stone pavilion that anchors one corner of the building.

As with a motorcycle, an industrial economy of materials is transmogrified into something sculptural and baroque. And fittingly for a museum dedicated to celebrating the accomplishments of the men and women of motorcycling, the building combines the human-scaled with the highway-scaled; it draws its form from both man and machine.

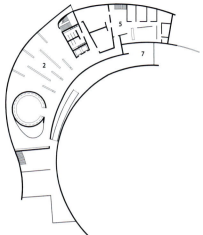

1 Entry
2 Gallery
3 Cafe / Store
4 Auditorium
5 Offices
6 Storage / Loading
7 Open to Below

Second Floor Plan

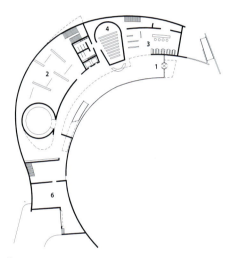

First Floor Plan

∧ Museum entry court with motorcycle parking.

∨ Curved rear of building inspired by motorcycle form.

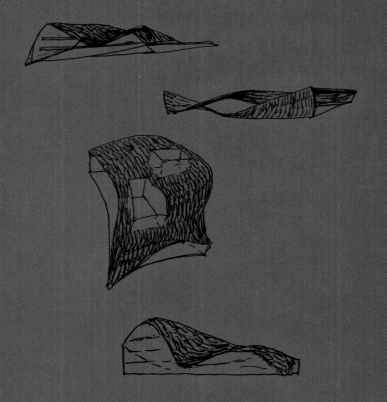

The sketchbooks may seem to make the visions extraterritorial, floating as they do on the white page. Yet it is, in fact, the site itself, in all its topographic, contextual and historical complexity, that works the design. After-images of ruminations may haunt the process obliquely, but the site must be an active agent in forming the concept. The building context is an asset that transports these ruminations from the general to the specific. Design remains open to external influence, and so opens the range of projects: they vary widely from site to site, design to design.

SENSITIVITY TO CONTEXT

CENTRALIZED DINING AND STUDENT SERVICES FACILITY
UNIVERSITY OF CALIFORNIA, BERKELEY

Berkeley, California

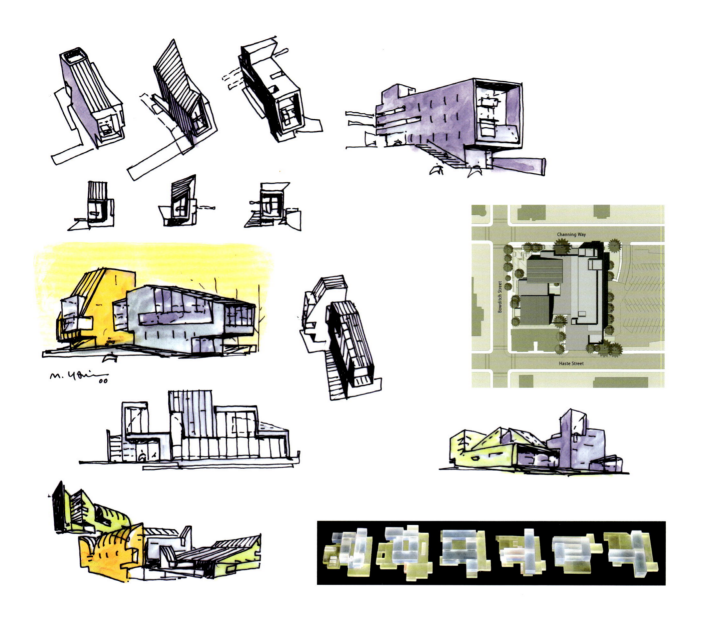

The Centralized Dining and Student Services Facility at the University of California, Berkeley, needed to blend two distinct programs—a dining hall and office tower—and two distinct contexts—historic craftsman houses and high-rise dormitories—in order to successfully integrate itself into a vibrant campus and neighborhood community. Through a layered approach to massing and fenestration, the building becomes stimulating and comfortable, and relates with its neighbors as a friendly and contemporary presence.

A six-foot drop in site level inspired a parti that accommodates the 90,000-square-foot building's bulk. In the front, low entrance pavilions create sheltered outdoor sitting and dining areas, while preserving the residential scale of the street. A series of stone steps and ramps connects the building with the sidewalk, while creating an intimate and clearly defined space for students to socialize in. The dining pavilions themselves weave around several mature pine trees that help to filter sunlight and maintain privacy, in conjunction with alternating clear and translucent glass. The main kitchen for the marche-style dining hall is tucked into the ground floor of the office building, which is pushed to the rear of the site to reduce the sense of its scale. Given their separate (although sometimes overlapping) clientele, the four-story tower has its own entrance at the side. Its mass is further broken down into a series of layers: offices are pushed to the long windowed edges, while the center of the building—expressed externally in vibrant ochre plaster—contains the support spaces. Fixed metal sunscreens turn a sustainable feature into a collage-like design element.

^ Dining facility entry plaza along Bowditch Street.

∧ Interior dining room view to entry.

> Dining patio along Bowditch Street.

○ Ground Floor Plan

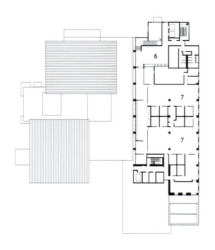

Typical Upper Floor Plan

1 Plaza / Dining Entry
2 Main Dining
3 Outdoor Dining
4 Kitchen / Servery
5 Student Services Entry
6 Reception
7 Offices
8 Storage / Loading

∧ Student Services building entry on Channing Way.

> Detail of Student Services building window wall.

< Outdoor dining patio.

GLENDALE POLICE HEADQUARTERS

Glendale, California

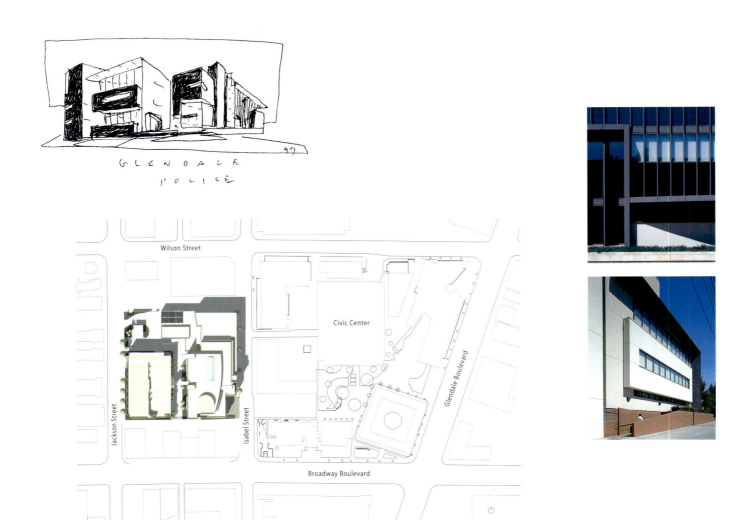

The Glendale Police Department's new facility finds its place in the stylistically crowded Glendale Civic Center district by abstractly responding to its context. Rather than being an Art Deco, Brutalist or Post-Modern building—as its neighbors are—it strives for timelessness by responding to elements of each style, while maintaining a contemporary attitude. The approach preserves the political importance of civic architecture and emphasizes urbanism—as both an enlivening of the street and an open attitude towards a historic environment.

This 263,000-square-foot building is massed to minimize its sense of bulk. With a mix of both public and private uses—including administrative offices, community assembly rooms, a jail, and a 911-dispatch center—the plan balances openness with security. The entrance is pulled to the corner to directly engage the Glendale City Hall, across the street, and is set in a stone pavilion that is visually distinct from the rest of the building. It is in the first in a series of design events that breaks down the overall mass: a stretch of curtain wall with vertically articulated mullions recalls City Hall's art deco character, without being explicitly historicist; and a tower of metal panels injects color into the composition and balances a more solid red stucco pavilion at the far end. The result is a contemporary collage that preserves a pedestrian-scaled environment by coming right up to the street edge. The entire fourth story is set back, in order to preserve the third floor cornice line of other structures on the street, while accommodating the program. On the interior, a two-story atrium space brings natural light deep into the building, and serves as a focal point for conference and break rooms, encouraging interaction.

An adjacent garage—while not typically a building type known for being a good neighbor—reacts to its surroundings with an abstract pattern of modular panels. The gray and green cast forms break up the façade into vertical masses, proportionately comparable to the design elements of apartment buildings along the street. The effort reveals the expectation that the entire project contribute to the life of Glendale's streets, fulfilling a civic need through both its program and design. The building succeeds in being both cohesive and contemporary—acknowledging the city's past while looking forward to the future.

∧∧ View south toward building entry on North Isabel Street.

∧ View north to building façade on North Isabel Street.

< Parking structure façade.

> Building entry detail.

CLARK COUNTY DETENTION CENTER

Las Vegas, Nevada

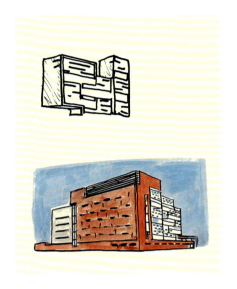

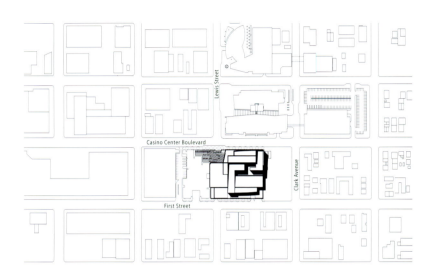

The Clark County Detention Center integrates an unwanted but necessary facility into Las Vegas' busy downtown cityscape. Located only a few blocks from casinos and entertainment areas, and adjacent to the federal and county courthouses, the building had to be a good neighbor—even as its program prohibits basic urbanistic gestures like entrances at street level.

The 320,000-square-foot facility, which adds thirteen hundred beds to an existing 1,400-bed jail, declares its programmatic elements with three distinct textures: the red concrete block houses administrative segregated cells, the tan plaster clads dormitory cells, and the patterned metal grills enclose outdoor recreation areas. The abstracted facades calm the rugged character of the building, while its vertical street walls maintain the scale of the neighborhood. One edge of the building is set behind a low pedestal, allowing light into administrative offices without sacrificing security. Aluminum butterfly screens on the cell windows prevent interaction between detainees and passersby while accommodating the requirement that each cell receive natural light. The perforated screens are a less expensive alternative to a reinforced window wall. Formally, they animate the unornamented facade of the cellblock, casting shadows across the wall.

With an architecture consisting entirely of cost-effective and durable materials, the detention center demonstrates the possibilities for high quality design in a situation typically afforded the lowest common denominator. Rather than being a monolithic, imposing facility, it creates an urbanistic and sculptural facade, on the cheap.

> Detail of rear façade at southwest edge of building.

v Front façade of main detention facility, along Casino Center Boulevard.

v
v Typical dormitory floor plan.

>> Detail of front façade.

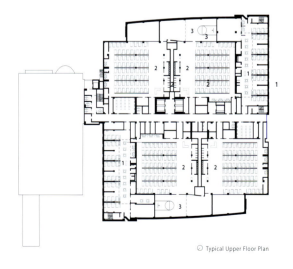

1 Admin. Segregation Cell Module
2 Dormitory Module
3 Covered Outdoor Exercise Yard

○ Typical Upper Floor Plan

SANTA MONICA PUBLIC SAFETY FACILITY

Santa Monica, California

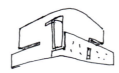

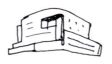

The design of the 113,000-square-foot headquarters for Santa Monica's police, fire and emergency operations emerged out of constraints: it had to accommodate round-the-clock activities in both highly secure and public areas; its height, setback and footprint had to adhere to the Santa Monica Civic Center master plan; and it had to be environmentally sustainable, earning a Silver LEED rating. From this difficult starting point rose a contemporary civic building that energizes its surroundings.

The design knits together a complicated multi-layered site by deploying a single palette of materials across a variety of scales. On the back side of the building, facing the Santa Monica freeway, the facade is a 200-foot-long monolithic sweep, meant to be experienced at highway speeds. It tapers to a sharp point, and is punctuated by an exit staircase encased in a steel cage extruded from the rear wall. In contrast, the front of the building consists of more human-scaled components that encourage pedestrian interaction and respond to the site's shifts in topography. A series of two to three story orthogonal volumes recalls the proportions of residential buildings – making the facility more approachable – while the corner tower serves as a vertical demarcation of the entire civic center campus, like a modern interpretation of a campanile. Two public spaces—one marking the entry and the other offering a view towards the ocean—are linked by a waterfall, which also masks the noise from the adjoining boulevard. While the primary building material throughout is ribbed concrete—like freeway paving—the entrance pavilion is ceremoniously dressed up in sandstone. Both materials react to Santa Monica's abundant sunshine with textures that change character as the light shifts over the course of the day.

The building's sustainable features accommodate stringent security requirements. Across the exterior, fixed sunshades block the harsh sun, while aesthetically animating the facade and signaling the building's commitment to energy efficiency. Small, secure balconies allow occupants to step out for fresh air. A three-story internal atrium and light shelves bring natural light deep into the building's large footprint. An under-floor air distribution system minimizes the amount of energy necessary to cool the building, while the moderate Santa Monica temperatures allow the use of large quantities of fresh, outside air, improving air quality. Throughout the building, materials were selected based on recycled content and renewable resources, with endangered woods and toxic materials eliminated.

The complex integrates law enforcement and public safety functions into a vibrant Civic Center. The building reinforces pedestrian paths, creates outdoor space for employees and the public, and defines the edges of the Civic Center—creating an upgraded image of the city's public facilities, and a showpiece of sustainability.

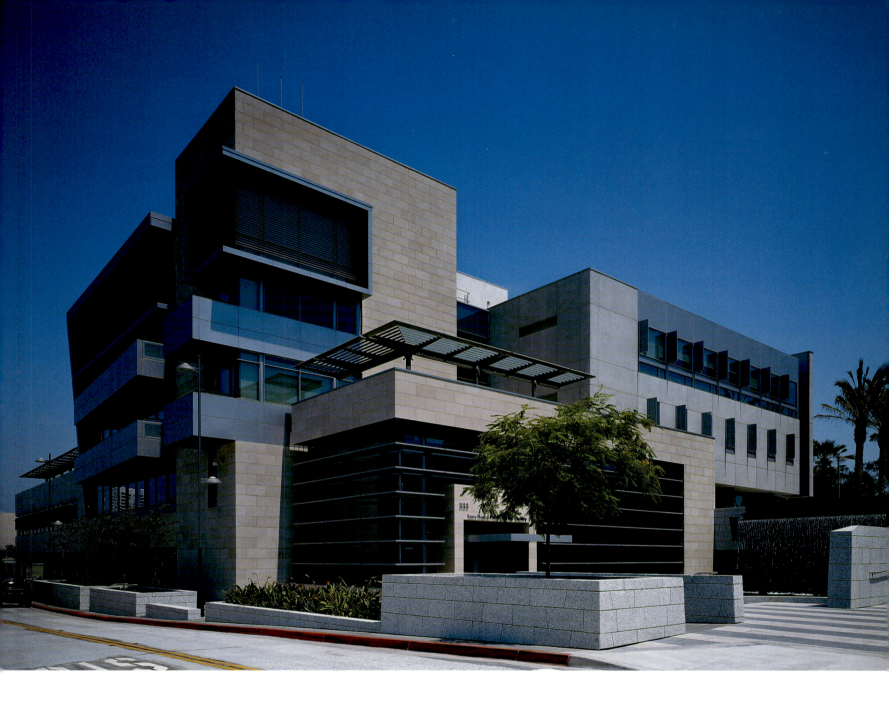

∧ View of building entry.

> Rear of building along the freeway.

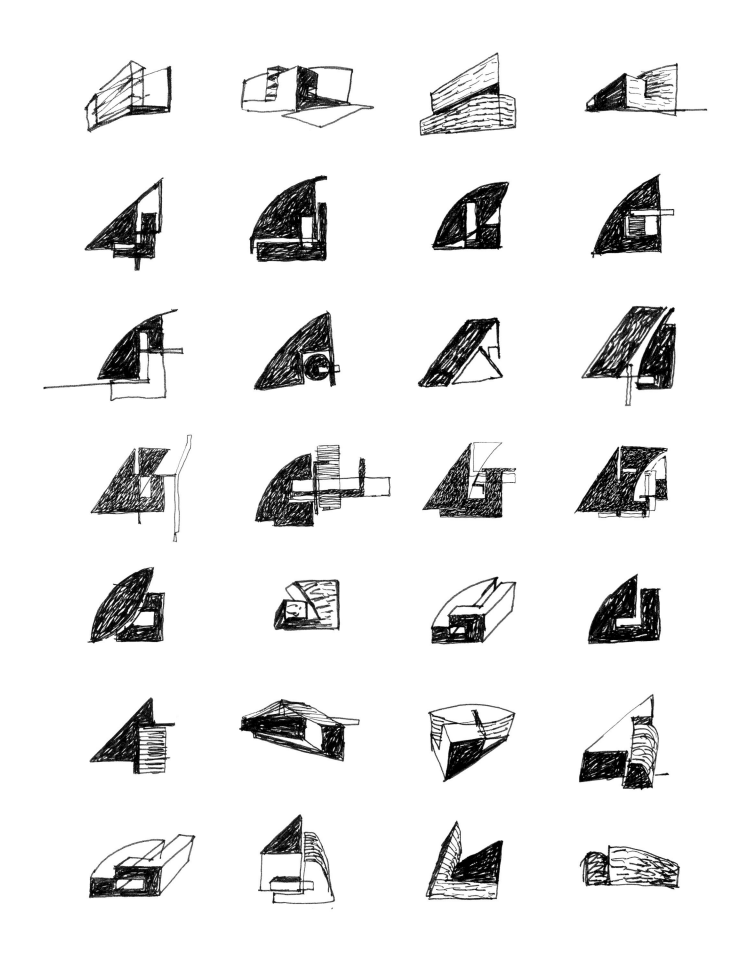

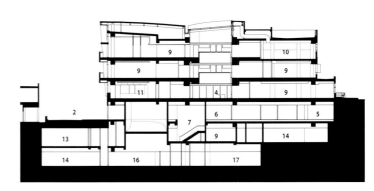

Section

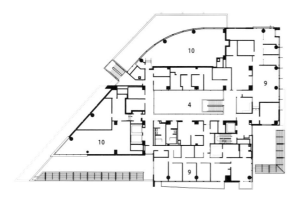

Fourth Floor Plan

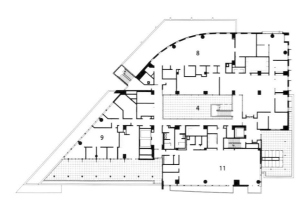

Second Floor Plan

1 Public Plaza
2 Plaza / Entry
3 Reception
4 Atrium
5 Records
6 Traffic / Parking
7 Operations / Administration
8 Fire Administration
9 Support Services / Offices
10 Mechanical
11 Community Room
12 Jail
13 Firing Range
14 Below Grade Drop-Off
15 Lockers
16 Dorm
17 Evidence

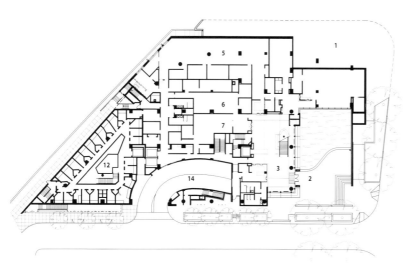

Ground Floor Plan

∧< Building section and floor plans.

> Building atrium.

∧ View of northeast facade and public plaza along Fourth Street.

< View from building entry toward Fourth Street plaza demonstrates design response to grade change.

<< Detail of building facade.

YESHIVA UNIVERSITY OF LOS ANGELES BOYS HIGH SCHOOL

Los Angeles, California

The Yeshiva University Boys High School brings the spirit of Jerusalem to a tight urban site along a busy boulevard in West Los Angeles. This private high school for two hundred students was designed to be constructed in two phases: phase one, already complete, involves the renovation of an existing office building into classrooms, art exhibition spaces, a conference facility, and a Beit Midrash, or religious library; phase two creates a symbolic center for the campus with a dramatic new library and gymnasium. The 50,000-square-foot facility is connected to the adjacent Museum of Tolerance by a bridge. When finished, the complex will encircle a cloister, creating a distinctive place for contemplation and socializing on a restricted site.

With budget constraints prohibiting the alteration of the existing floor plate, the original building's character was refreshed by creating small window incisions in the facade. The walls of the Beit Midrash were pushed out to bring light to the Bima, or altar, while a corner window washes the walls with light, emphasizing the texture of the Jerusalem-stone walls. In the exhibition wing, a stair landing pops through the facade, its glowing sculptural form becoming a punctuation mark for the primary entrance axis of the campus. The library, to be built in the second phase of construction, is the most formally ambitious part of the program. Its sculpted, fragmented form will be clad in copper shingles, marking it as the campus' focal point. The remaining facades are finished with white stucco, providing an ascetic clarity reminiscent of Mediterranean architecture.

The overall intent is to summon the sense of being in Jerusalem without resorting to clichés or stylistic motifs. The combination of the smooth surfaces of white plaster against the blue California sky, Jerusalem stone, and a landscaping program of olive and cypress trees creates that feeling—while hewing to a contemporary, at times abstract, architectural spirit.

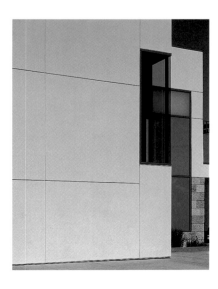

< ∧ Courtyard view to exhibition wing.

∧> Rear courtyard and entry to classroom buildings.

>> Detail contrasts white plaster with Jerusalem stone.

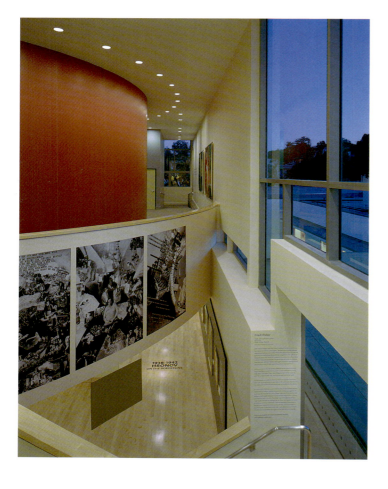

∧ The school's exhibit space and auditorium are accessible from the adjacent Museum of Tolerance.

OXNARD HOUSE

Oxnard, California

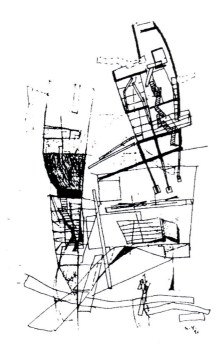

The design for the Oxnard house, on the Pacific coast north of Los Angeles, is a monument to California's conflicted spirit, a whimsical mediation between the artificial and the natural. Rather than hugging the contours of its sloping two-acre site, it rises vertically to suggest an alternative relationship between architecture and the landscape. The house is itself a window, a framing device that reminds us that the landscape is a shared creation of both humans and nature. Its height minimizes its footprint while maximizing the occupants' sense of their relationship to the surroundings.

Designed as a second home for a couple from Los Angeles, who planned to eventually make it their primary residence, the building is approached on a series of ramps that rise up from the slope to meet the facade at its center-point. With the entryway set in the donut-like hole, the architecture immediately states its intention of connecting to the landscape by framing the view. The four-story house is composed of two main volumes, one metal, one translucent glass, that join at the central void. Living areas are on the upper level, with a garage, guest rooms and studio below. The curved forms of the skin are inspired by the contours of the land, and reflect the softness and organic nature of the site.

The Oxnard house presents a broader view of the best way for architecture to fit into the landscape. It isn't meant to be a collision with nature but a collage of materials and perspectives, land and architecture. The vertical design may make the building assertive in some ways, yet it also allows it to touch the land as lightly as possible, and frame the landscape. Its provocative ideas and forms have led to the inclusion of the model in the Museum of Modern Art's permanent collection.

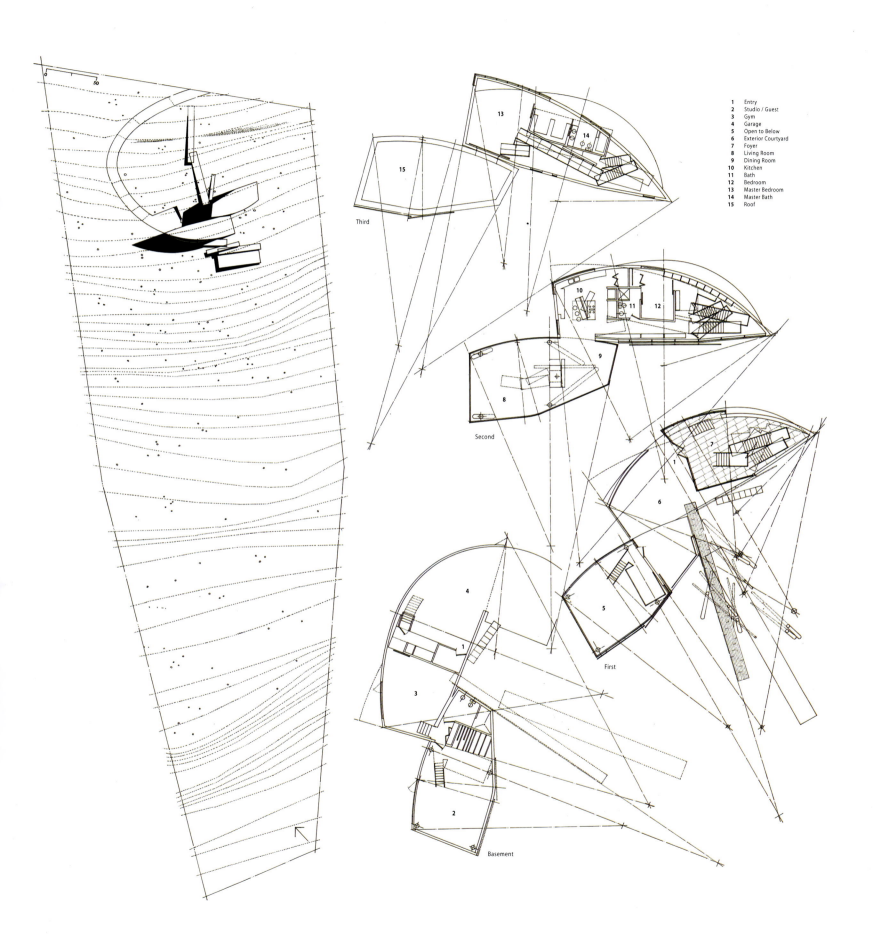

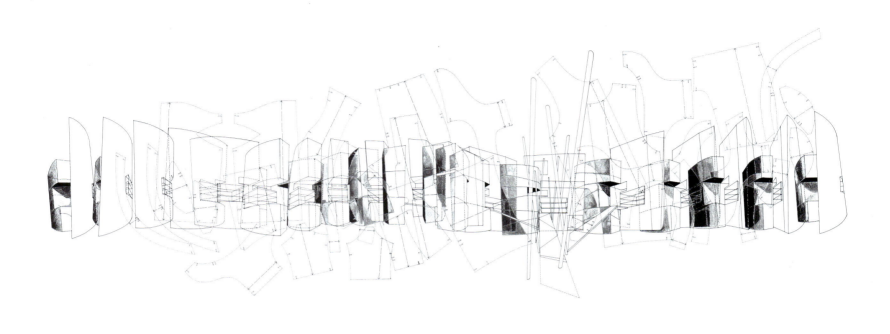

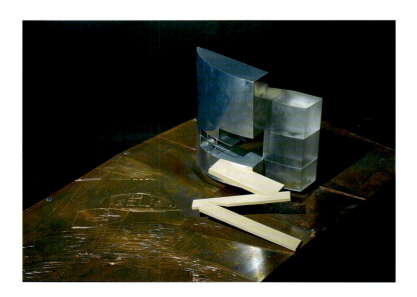

∧ Diagram illustrates 360° views in multiple stages.

<> Presentation model – front and rear of house.

TOMIHIRO MUSEUM OF SHI-GA COMPETITION

Gunma Prefecture, Japan

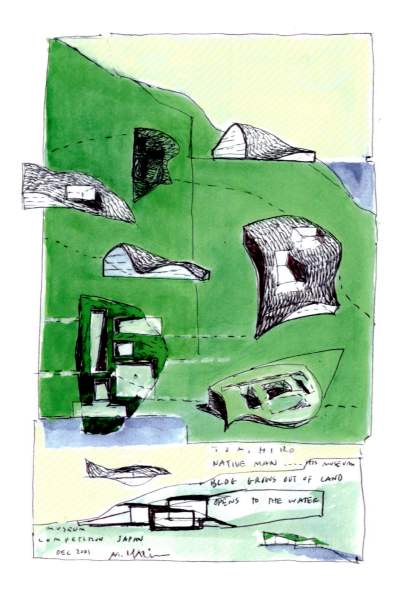

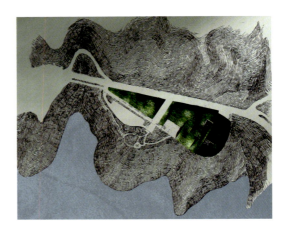

The design for the Tomihiro Museum in Gunma Prefecture, Japan, responds to both the narrative and physical contexts of its site. The museum replaces an existing building celebrating the artist Tomihiro Hoshino, a physical education teacher who turned to art after he became paralyzed. As art helped Tomihiro heal himself, so the new museum would celebrate his work while healing the surrounding landscape of the damage done by an earlier museum, whose construction leveled the crest of the hillside.

The form of the new building was developed by using topographic models of the site to recreate the contours of the hillside, which are then expressed in the curves of the sod-covered roof. Natural light enters the building through slits, glazed in colored glass, cut into the concrete roof-deck. The result is a mix of light spectrums against the gallery walls, creating a poetic reflection of Tomihiro's use of watercolors, with their varying levels of transparency and color. The intimately-scaled galleries form a clear progression, creating a physical path through the exhibit's narrative of Tomihiro's life. The gallery spaces also acknowledge the curves of the roof, so that visitors are continually linked back to the topography of the site.

The Tomihiro Museum demonstrates a broader, more narrative-based approach to the notion that a building should be sensitive to its context. Not only does it relate to its physical setting, but it responds to the widest range of factors affecting the project, including the history of the site and the stories it contains.

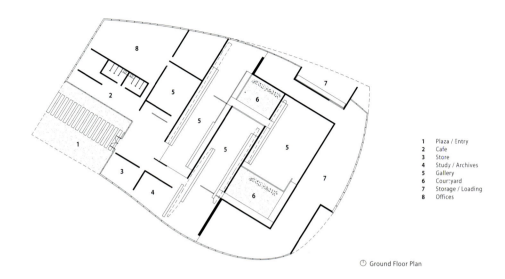

1 Plaza / Entry
2 Cafe
3 Store
4 Study / Archives
5 Gallery
6 Courtyard
7 Storage / Loading
8 Offices

Ground Floor Plan

v   Museum facade is glazed to provide maximum views of the water beyond.

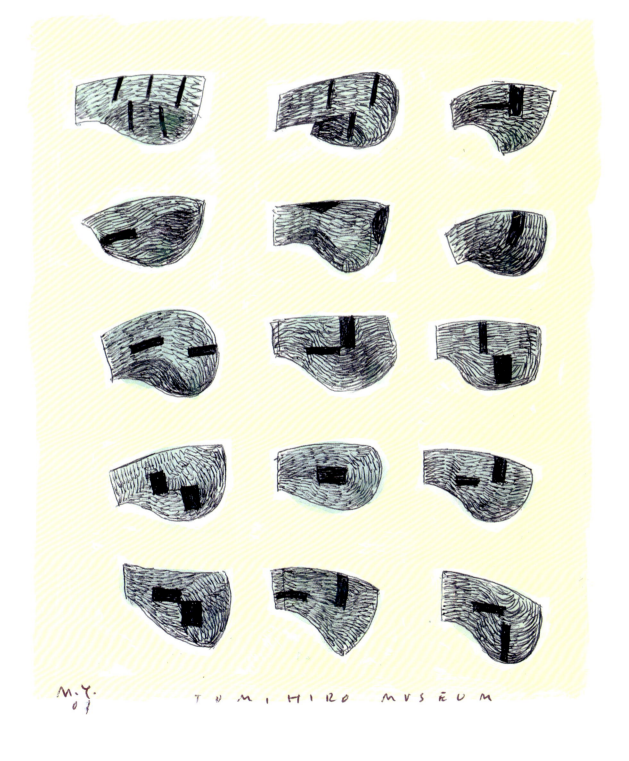

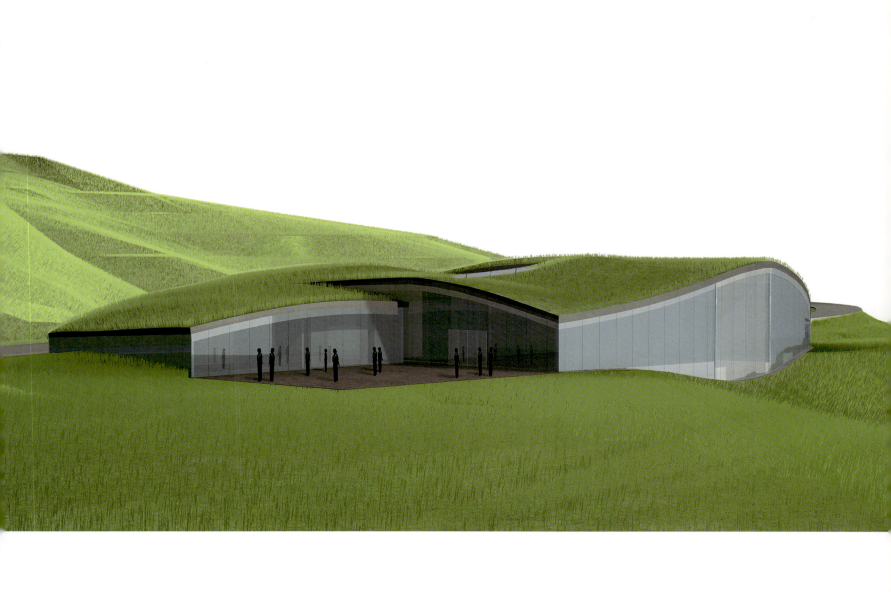

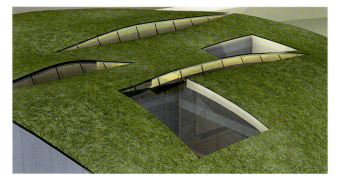

< Plan studies.

∧ Building form is integrated into hillside.

> Roof detail.

∧ > Renderings of connections between indoor gallery and outdoor spaces.

Interspersed among the abstract studies are generative designs, explorations in plan, section, perspective and diagram for buildings on the boards. At times, these ruminations evolve with projects, as studies and visions are integrated into the complexities of the commissions, in a reflexive process of imagining and making.

INTEGRATING SKETCHES

SHOWSCAN CINEMANIA THEATER

Universal City, California

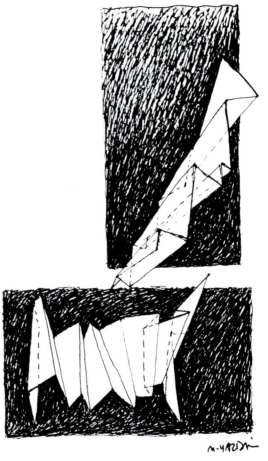
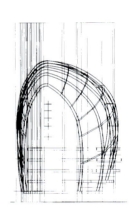

The Showscan Theater for Universal City Walk at Universal Studios inserts real architecture between two simulated environments. The surrounding streetscape is a theme park simulacrum with stage-set facades hiding empty buildings; the theater itself provides an immersive simulated experience created by a fifty-foot curved screen set before hydraulically operated seats. But between them is an architectural experiment in creating a threshold for the transition from reality to make-believe.

The experiment begins with the marquee, where traditional signage is replaced with a warped and folded fiberglass plane that floats, cloud-like, above the entrance. At night it becomes an electronic billboard like others on the simulated street, except that the folds in the fiberglass blur the rear-projection image, giving visitors the first clue to the reality-bending experience waiting for them inside. During the day, the projections go dark and the potato chip-like folds of the marquee assert their tectonic dynamism, as a deliberate affront to the theater's cardboard neighbors. The lower half of the curved facade is finished in a luminescent Venetian plaster that again emphasizes its reality via its materiality, and serves as a backdrop to the ticket holders lining up along it.

Since the technical requirements of the theater demanded a plain box, the lobby becomes the primary architectural opportunity for impacting the visitors' experience. Conceived as a decompression chamber between a reality of simulations (Universal City Walk) and a simulated reality (the film), it redefines expected architectural elements. The curved walls meet at their tops, eliminating a conventional ceiling; a steel deck platform suspends visitors in the air, eliminating a conventional floor; light washes up the walls from an unseen source, eliminating conventional illumination. Two sculpted columns crash through the space, playing off the room's ovoid form, while the handrails are fabricated in glass.

The overall effect is that of a gray zone between the false reality of outside, and the other reality of the film within. The experience is confounding—a fitting sensation for a building whose internal spaces do not match the experiences they contain.

∧ Box office and entry.

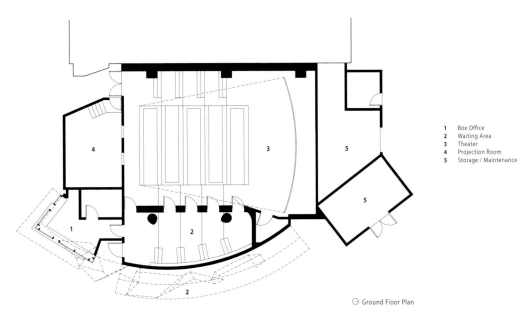

1 Box Office
2 Waiting Area
3 Theater
4 Projection Room
5 Storage / Maintenance

⊖ Ground Floor Plan

∧ Theater waiting area interior.

< Illuminated view of building.

ROYAL THEATER PLAYHOUSE COMPETITION

Copenhagen, Denmark

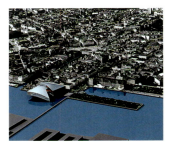

As a new landmark building for Copenhagen, the Royal Theater of Denmark seeks to revitalize the waterfront and integrate it into the historic fabric of the city. Its location at the southern end of Kvaesthusbroen—facing the new opera house across the water, but not encroaching on the existing pier—energizes the development of a waterfront park and leaves space for an outdoor theater. This siting follows the grid of the historic city and maintains the urban block size, but does not break it down into smaller units. Instead, it celebrates the theater as a civic monument by occupying the block with a single form whose innovative glazing system gives the building a character simultaneously monolithic and gauzy.

An outdoor public plaza replaces a grand street-level lobby as the theater's ceremonial entrance. From there, a series of escalators sweeps theatergoers through a gap between two wedges of the building, angled to create a visual connection with the new opera house. The main public gathering space is upstairs, seemingly hovering above the water, adjoined by a smaller café space that dips back down towards the plaza level. In plan, the building's two theaters are orthogonally arranged, but volumetrically their relationship is abstracted, giving the building its distinctive swooping curves. A glass and perforated metal skin reveals the activity within the building to the street, at varying levels of transparency—like a theater's scrim.

The building's dramatic forms and ethereal glazing contrast with the historic urban backdrop, reinforcing it as a civic landmark. But it also becomes a commentary on the role of arts in the city: the theater is designed as a series of spatial events, so that the experience of moving through it is theatrical, even before one reaches the performance space itself. By choreographing this transition from city to stage, the building encourages reflection on the classic notion of art informing life, and life informing art.

∧ View of building forms from water.

∨ Massing studies.

 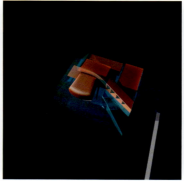 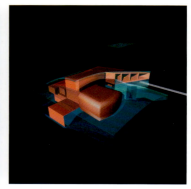

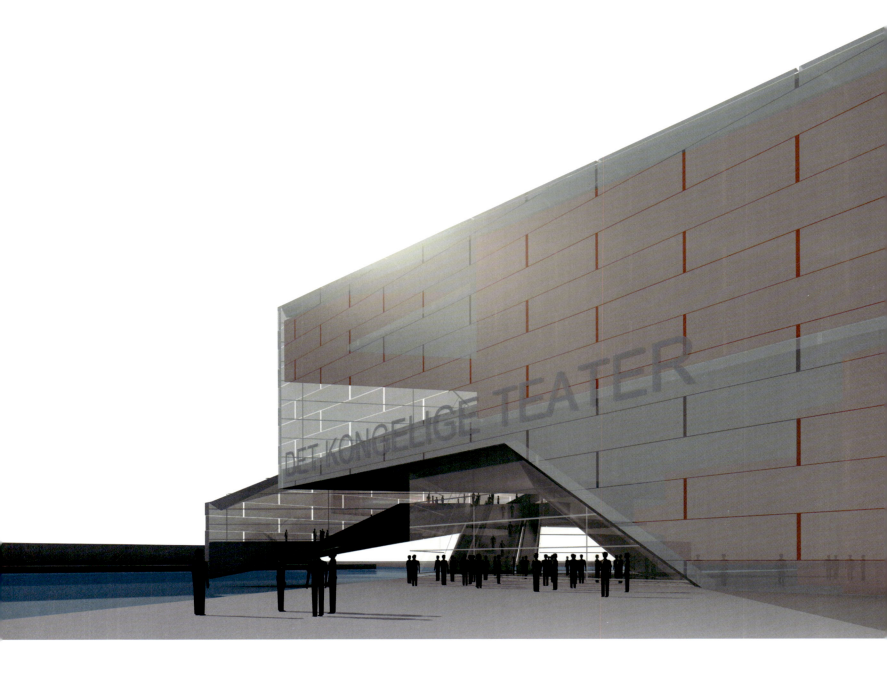

∧ Entry plaza.

< Study models.

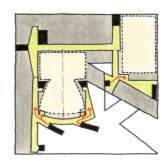

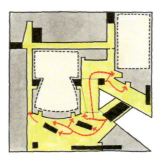

> Plan diagrams.

v View of playhouse from Copenhagen Harbor.

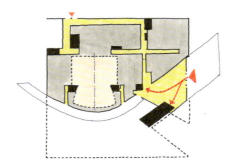

QUEENSLAND GALLERY OF MODERN ART

Brisbane, Australia

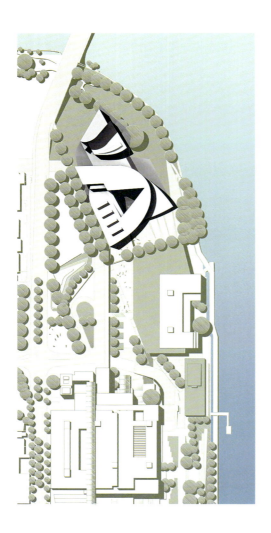

The design of the Queensland Gallery of Modern Art suggests that the experiences of urban life and viewing art can exist in a continuous relationship. Contrary to the tendency to set museums apart and seal them off from the city, the spiral form of the gallery emphasizes its connection to the urban milieu, and reflects its charge of helping to revitalize the South Bank area of Brisbane as an arts precinct.

The gallery was inspired by a spiraling seashell, which suggested possibilities for rethinking conventional thresholds between indoors and out. The dramatically black-clad planes of the spiral open to accept the public promenade rising up into the gallery. In place of a lobby, the central hall serves as the meeting place for both visitors and the community, and is animated by cinemas, a gift shop and café. At its center rises a spiraling ramp that creates a consistent reference point for the building, without eliminating the opportunity for exploration and discovery. A continuous path from an outdoor plaza into the central hall and up through a sequence of exhibition spaces demonstrates the continuity of experience from the street to the art. Yet the sequence of galleries is arranged so that visitors can either follow a rigid path or explore on their own—creating a playful tension between random activity and an organized museum visit.

The design demonstrates a new way of thinking about the relationship of art and architecture at a museum: a building can have a strong presence while remaining inviting to the public and materially connected to the city. Recognizing the appeal of the waterfront boardwalk as a civic space, the design conceives of the building as a continuation of that experience, becoming a metaphor for the ways in which art is a continuation of urban life.

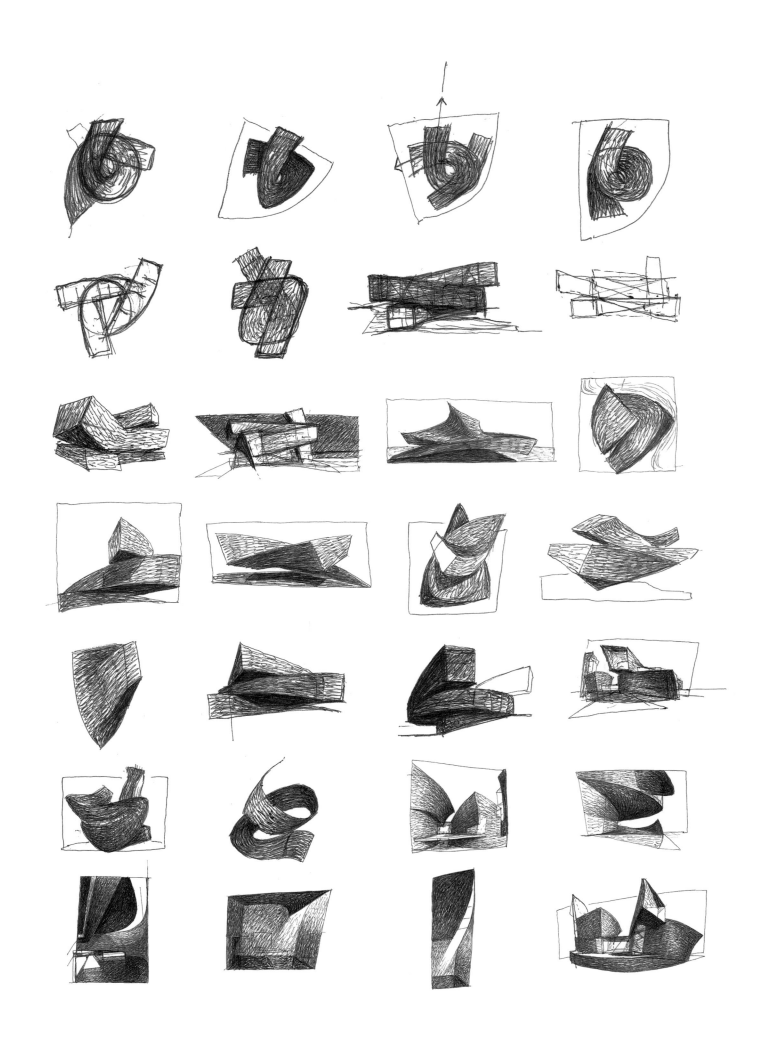

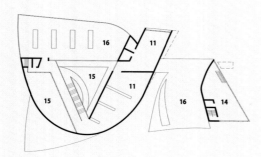

Third Floor Plan

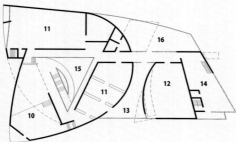

1 Plaza / Entry
2 Information
3 Atrium
4 Bookstore
5 Cafe
6 Theater
7 Outdoor Ampitheater
8 Curatorial / Storage
9 Loading
10 Temporary Exhibitions
11 Gallery
12 Sculpture Gallery
13 Sculpture Terrace
14 Offices
15 Open to Below
16 Roof

Second Floor Plan

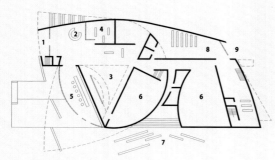

⊖ Ground Floor Plan

< Preliminary sketches.

> View of buildings from southwest end of complex.

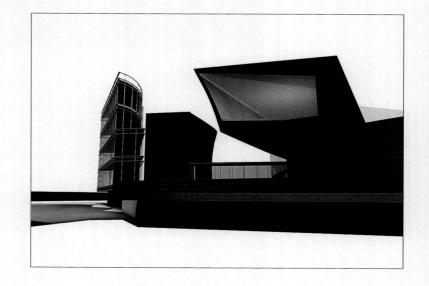

OVERLAND HOUSE

Los Angeles, California

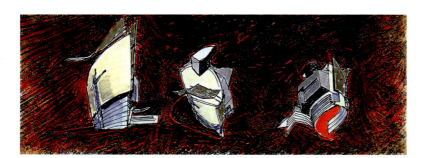

The design of the Overland House and Studio takes its form from the visual language common to the architect and his wife, a fashion designer: the two-dimensional shapes from which three-dimensional forms emerge. The house was designed as an accessory building for a lot in West Los Angeles, replacing an existing garage. Its 1,300 square feet are spread over a two-story high volume, with kitchen and living spaces on the ground level, connected by a spiral staircase to a bedroom and study, and topped by a rooftop terrace.

    The design explores the idea that clothing patterns and architectural plans are both abstractions responding to a common concern for how the human figure inhabits its environment. The intersecting planes of the building's plan and section were developed through a series of collages and sketches that began with the image of a piece of fabric draped over a bodice—the seminal three-dimensional exercise in the creation of a two-dimensional pattern. Accordingly, the building's curves recall the human body, albeit mediated by the two-dimensional language of the clothing pattern. The result becomes a celebration of the human figure as the common root of architecture and fashion.

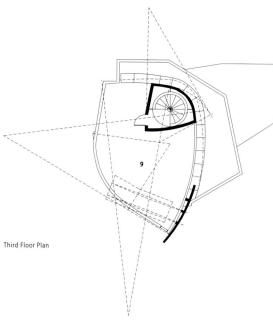

Third Floor Plan

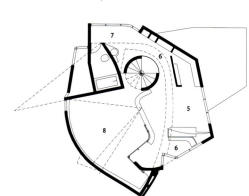

Second Floor Plan

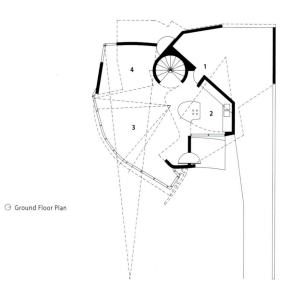

Ground Floor Plan

< Floor plans.

v Four views of building model.

1 Entry
2 Kitchen
3 Living Room
4 Dining Room
5 Bedroom
6 Closet
7 Bathroom
8 Open to Below
9 Rooftop Garden

v   Fragments of exterior facades.

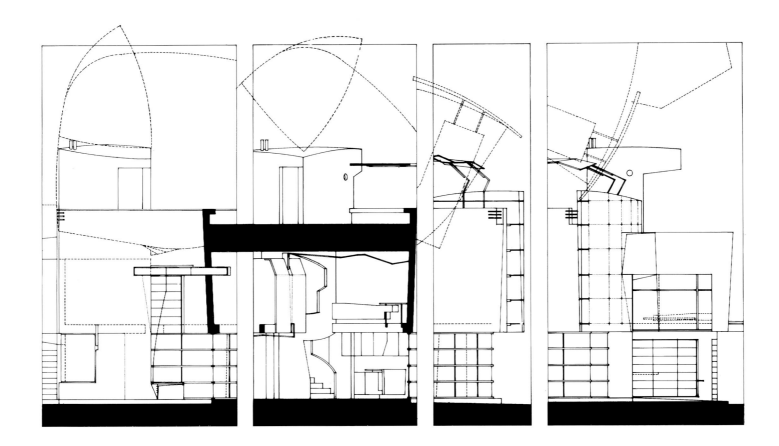

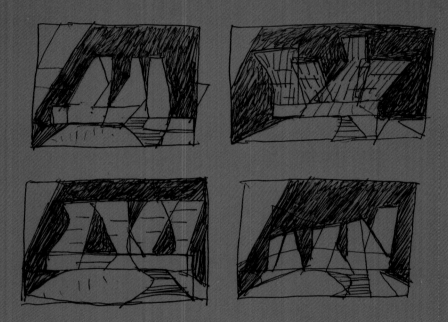

Too often, public buildings actually limit public access and use, when they should be reaching out to instill in the general populace a degree of intellectual engagement, of curiosity. This interaction may arise from a design gesture or a programmatic element – either of which is often an addition to the client's conception of the project. As a result of these augmentations and amenities, people can engage the spaces emotionally, or at least functionally, and those who would not have noticed or cared are now involved in their built environment.

PUBLIC ENGAGEMENT

LLOYD D. GEORGE UNITED STATES COURTHOUSE AND FEDERAL BUILDING

Las Vegas, Nevada

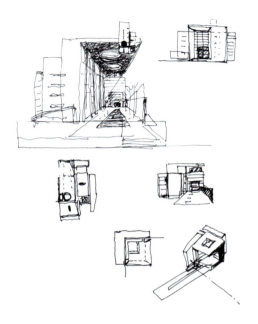
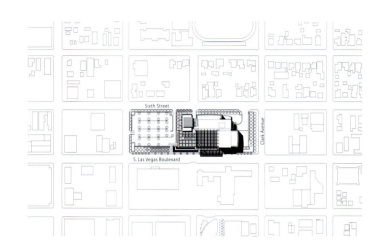

Las Vegas architecture is not typically known for its sense of gravitas and civic ideals, but that was exactly the mandate for the design of the Lloyd D. George United States Courthouse and Federal Building, located just a few miles from the Las Vegas Strip. As a prominent example of the General Services Administration's attempt at raising the quality of public architecture, the courthouse was one of the early commissions awarded under the Federal Design Excellence Program. The result is the rare federal building that is simultaneously accessible and secure, monumental and inviting; it cultivates public life by creating a space that can belong to both the judges who occupy it and the people whom it serves.

The courthouse defines itself as an important civic building and a symbolic center of the community by exchanging Las Vegas' typical artifice and impermanence for solidity and transparency. The design accommodates intense programmatic requirements without appearing fortress-like, or alienating the public. Its 437,000 square feet of facilities (serving the U.S. Courts for the District of Nevada, U.S. Marshall Services, and U.S. Senators) are configured in an L-shape set on a high plinth, simultaneously signaling the elevated ideals of the institution and providing the separation from the street necessary for security. By raising the outdoor plaza atop a staircase, it remains accessible but protected. A distinctive 175-foot-tall tapering steel column supports a metal canopy that shades the building from the desert sun and references the porticos of traditional courthouse architecture. Beneath it, an entrance rotunda emerges from the main building as a separate form, bringing ceremony to the process of entering the building and passing through security.

The symbolic connection between community and court continues inside. Circulation through a glass skin allows for a constant visual connection to the outdoor plaza and, by extension, the public. The juror assembly room is a distinct volume naturally lit by clerestory windows and opening onto a secure outdoor courtyard. In perhaps the clearest evidence that the design of the courthouse has created a new public space that welcomes the community and inspires civic pride, the room has become a meeting place for local organizations—a far cry from the basement purgatory typical of juror assembly rooms. It indicates the ways in which this building helped returns public engagement to the architecture of both Las Vegas' and federal courthouses.

∧ Entry plaza.

∨ Shade from plaza canopy shifts throughout the day with the sun's movement.

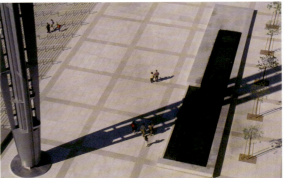

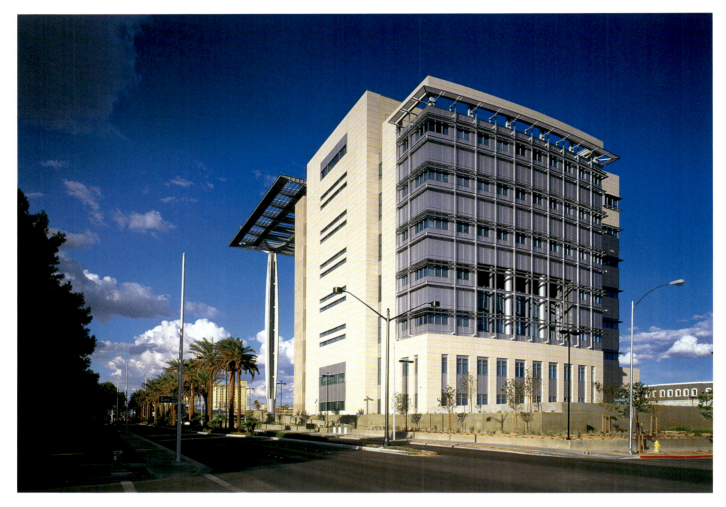

∧ Views of courthouse along Las Vegas Boulevard.

> Window wall detail.

< Courthouse entry rotunda.

> Exterior rotunda window.

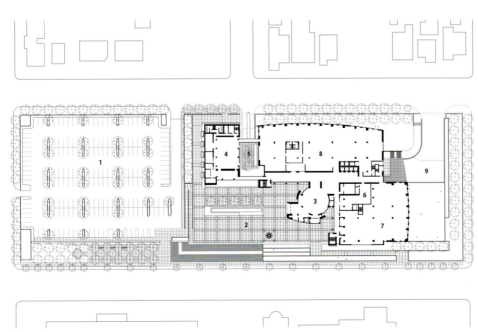

○ Ground Floor Plan

1 Parking
2 Public Plaza
3 Rotunda
4 Jury Assembly
5 Courtyard
6 Cafeteria
7 Offices
8 Court Clerk
9 Loading Area

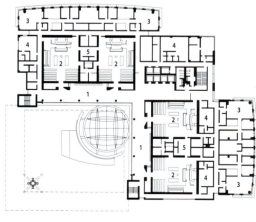

1 Public Corridor
2 Magistrate Courtroom
3 Judges Chambers
4 Jury Room
5 Holding Cell

^^ Elevator lobby of courtroom floor.

^ Courtroom interior.

> Typical floor plan.

>> Detail of rotunda skylight.

BEVERLY HILLS PUBLIC WORKS BUILDING AND WATER TREATMENT FACILITY

Los Angeles, California

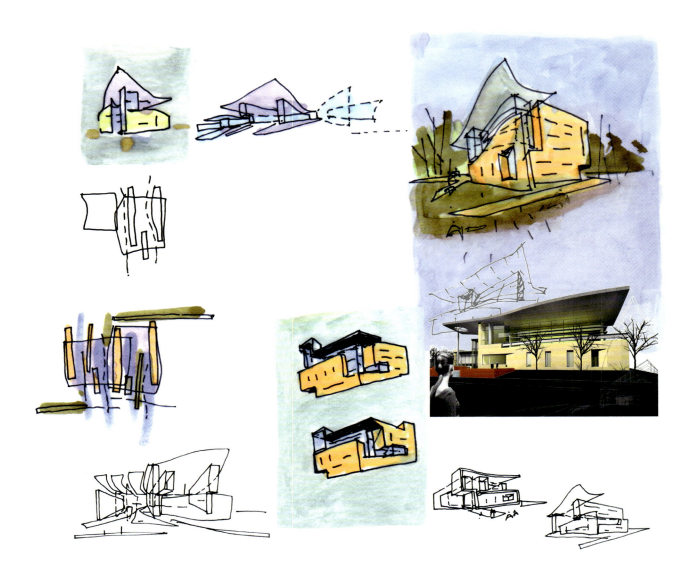

The compact and affluent community of Beverly Hills has no outskirts, meaning that its new water treatment plant would necessarily have to be built in plain sight. But out of this necessity emerged an opportunity for architectural enrichment and civic engagement. Developed as the first Design/Build/Finance/Operate public works building in California, the Beverly Hills Public Works and Reverse Osmosis Treatment Facility not only treats water, but raises infrastructure to the realm of public space.

The design creates a quiet but distinguished character for the 32,000-square-foot building, which is located in a mixed residential and commercial area. Rather than emphasizing security, the layout, massing and materials are oriented towards the sidewalk and the city. A glass entrance lantern, overhung by a wave-shaped elliptical roof, reveals the activity within to passersby. An elliptical multi-purpose room, dramatically clad in undulating u-channel glass, extends this idea with a direct visual connection to the water plant itself, allowing school groups and the general public to learn about the source of their water. The room is available for meetings or receptions appropriate to an environment symbolically connected to the life of the city. A small outdoor amphitheater, echoing the curves of the multi-purpose room, provides a place both for performances and sitting. At its center, an animated water feature is a literal and playful celebration of water. Extensive use of polished Jerusalem stone and glass throughout the building evokes the elements of a creek while maintaining a modern character.

The resulting building involves citizens with the systems that sustain their city. Included in the program was an exhibit on the history of water in Southern California—furthering the goal of making a facility that is typically opaque to public understanding both functional and educational. Just as in Renaissance Rome fountains celebrated the water supply as a necessary element of public life, the building demonstrates Beverly Hills' commitment to a positive vision of the future through environmental and economic sustainability.

∧ View of building façade and entry along Foothill Drive.

> Interior of water treatment facility.

< Interior of demonstration room.

v Detail of demonstration room curved glass wall, with lobby beyond.

> Plan.

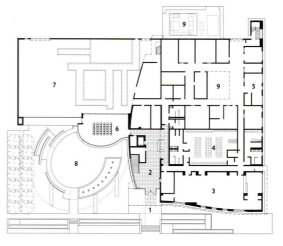

Ground Floor Plan

1 Entry / Plaza
2 Lobby
3 Cafeteria
4 Lockers
5 Offices
6 Demonstration Room
7 Water Treatment Plant
8 Courtyard
9 Storage

∧ >   Building entry and lobby.

LOS ANGELES METRO RED LINE STATION, VERMONT AVENUE/SANTA MONICA BOULEVARD

Los Angeles, California

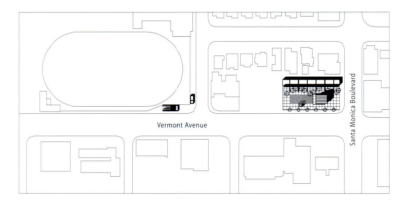

The presence of the subway in Los Angeles is incongruous enough; making a 30-foot metal canopy leap out of the sidewalk above the Metro Rail Station at the corner of Vermont Avenue and Santa Monica Boulevard is a particularly, and deliberately, striking surprise. The elliptical form is a civic-minded exclamation that rises above the adjacent taco stands and gas stations to declare as public space the plaza it dominates. Its stainless steel form—like a robust, L.A. version of Hector Guimard's Paris Metro signs—becomes a billboard for urban dignity, inviting the public to experience the station as a work of architecture. The broad street-level plaza is further animated by six leaning fire-engine-red light standards that seem to dance across the space, while the glass walls of the elevator cabin are similarly shifted off-axis.

Below ground, concrete becomes the canvas. The cavernous escalator passage is stenciled with 10,000 written questions, developed in collaboration with the Los Angeles artist Robert Millar, that coyly reflect on the design process of the station. The ceiling is perforated with glass pavers, allowing light to filter in from the plaza above, and the concrete crossbeams are affixed with colored florescent tubes that bring a hint of playfulness to the industrial space. The 450-foot-long train platform itself was conceived as a concrete tube filled with functional elements to emphasize the sensation of space carved from solid ground. All of the interventions are additive: the ticketing concourse seems to float within the main volume of the platform, air conduits reach out from the walls, and ceiling baffles disperse the artificial light. Most surfaces are clad in stainless steel, both to reflect light and stand up to vandals. This is tough architecture for tough conditions, but there is also an insistent dignity in its monumentality.

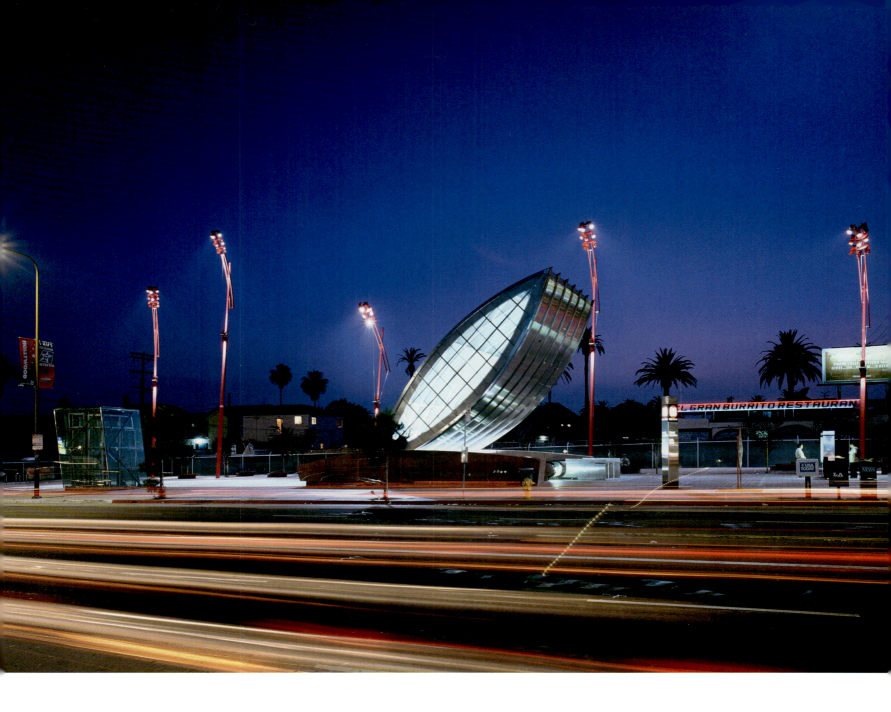

∧ Station entrance along Vermont Avenue.

> View of entry canopy and glass elevator bay from plaza at street level.

v Exploded axonometric diagram of track bed and platform.

\> Canopy detail and entry at night.

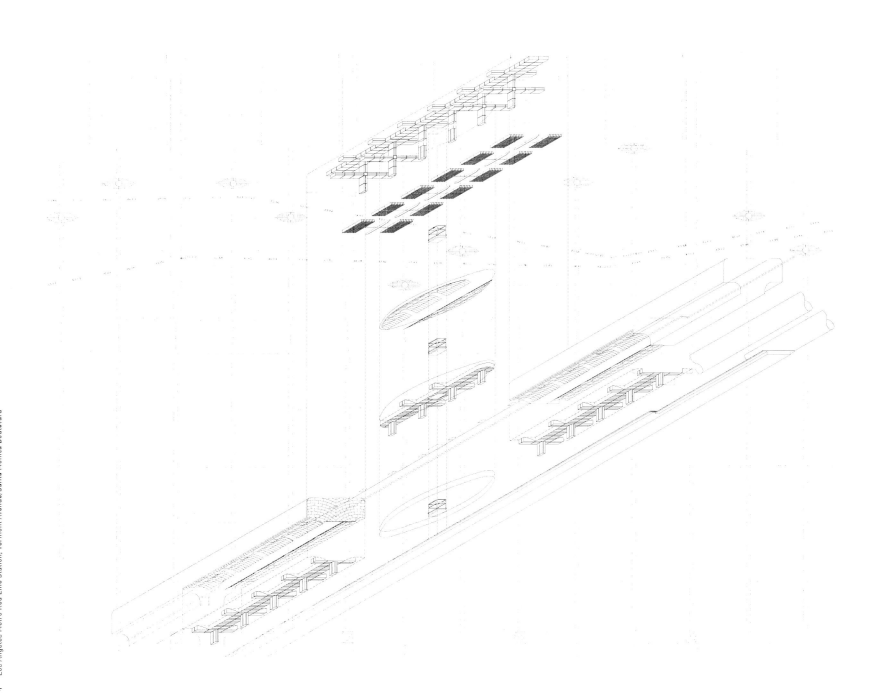

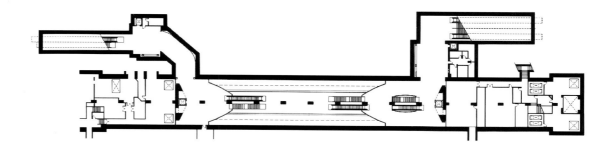

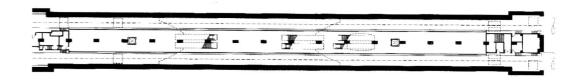

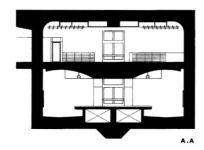

A.A

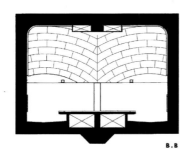

B.B

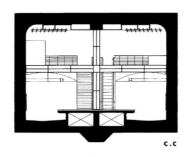

C.C

∧ Plans.

< Sections.

<< Passage to mezzanine level lit by glass pavers at street level.

Text painted on concrete walls by artist Robert Millar.

<^ Views of train platforms.

\> Ceiling detail illustrates perforated baffles.

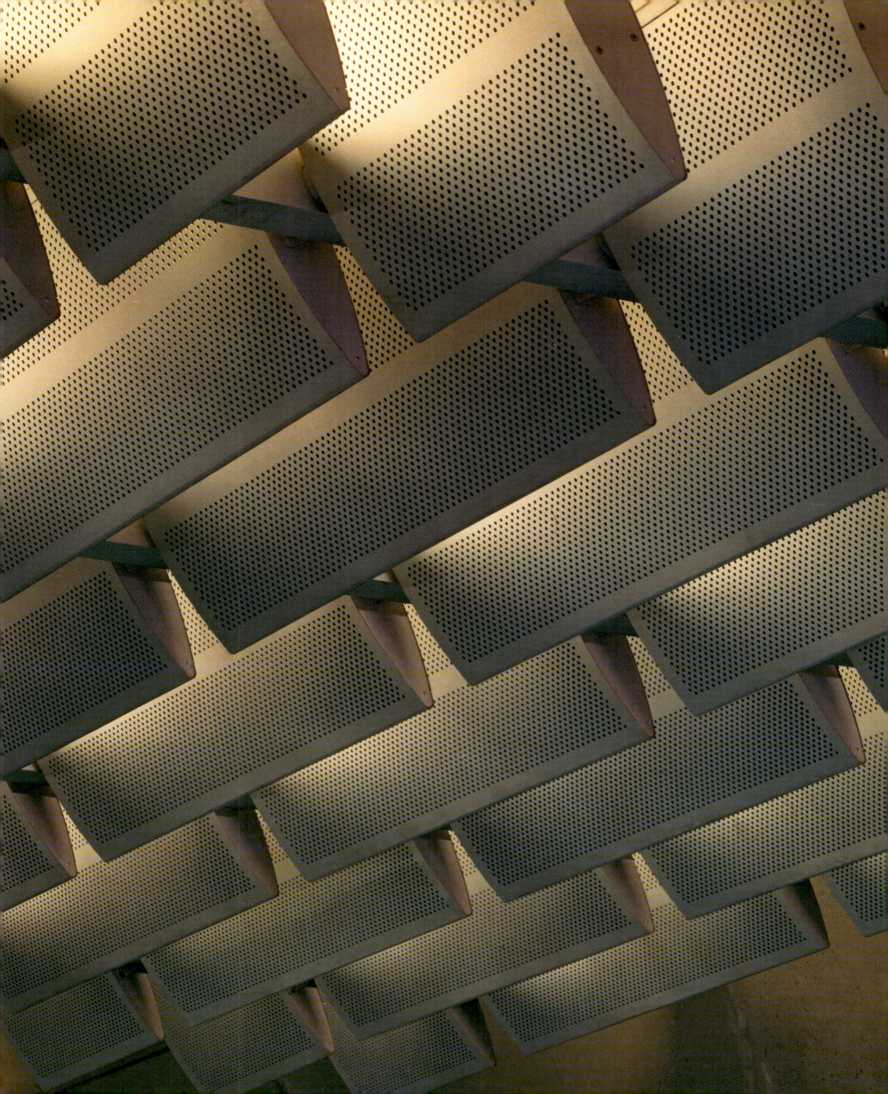

DUXTON PLAIN PUBLIC HOUSING COMPETITION

Singapore

The incredible pace of Singapore's growth demands innovative architectural solutions in order to prevent the wholesale replacement of green space with housing density. The competition entry for the Duxton Plain Public Housing project responds by modulating the organic nature of the site and the encroaching city. The site plan clusters the residential towers on the portion of the site nearest existing development, matching its neighbors in scale and proportion while leaving the remaining two-thirds available for green space. This configuration enables connections with the adjoining Duxton Plain Park, engages the existing public space, and unifies the existing urban fabric.

    The towers' shapes similarly reflect the organic nature of the site, as if creating an architectural foil between city and nature. The tapering and undulating forms break down the buildings into smaller elements of two to eight apartments per floor, eliminating the blandness and monotony typical of high-rise housing projects and creating unexpected opportunities for natural light and ventilation, including sky-gardens. The forms also allow for additional public space—such as community rooms and childcare facilities—to be brought up into the towers, encouraging the feeling of a neighborhood and maintaining a connection with the ground. The plan balances the megalopolis' need for both density and livability by creating a vertical community of variety, individuality and abundant public space.

v Housing is broken into three masses incorporating residential components with public/shared program spaces.

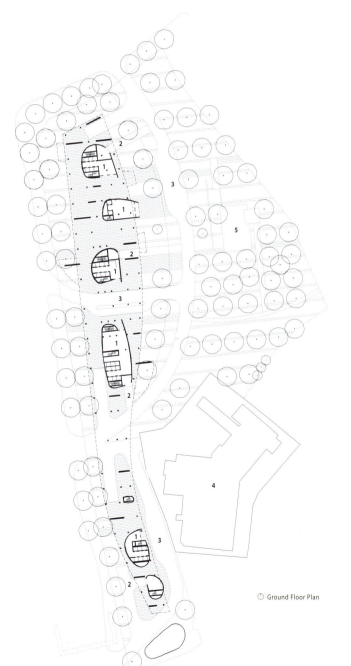

Ground Floor Plan

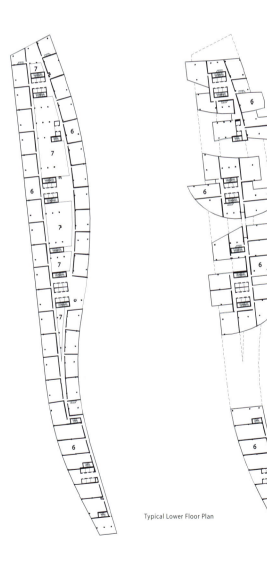

Typical Lower Floor Plan

Typical Upper Floor Plan

1 Lobby
2 Service Dock
3 Main Drop-Off
4 Community Center
5 Playground
6 Dwelling Units
7 Open to Below

GUANGZHOU TV AND SIGHTSEEING TOWER COMPETITION

Guangzhou, China

The design of the 540-metre-tall Guangzhou Television and Sightseeing Tower is derived from the symbolic form for the city itself. The Chinese character for "Guangzhou" is three flowing strokes around isolated dots, representing the three rivers that pass through the city. The building dramatically mimics this form, with three curving towers wrapping around crystal-shaped observation decks. The result is an iconic physical landmark for the city that embodies the spiritual implication of infinite harmony.

The poetic geometry of the tower begins with two overlapping equilateral triangles, which form three solid towers and a central "void tower." The elevation is driven by the same logic: the tower is vertically divided into three sections, each of which is divided three times, resulting in nine sections each sixty meters high. Like the scales on a piano keyboard, the repeating progression contains within it the possibility of the infinite—a sense emphasized by reflecting pools at the tower's base, which create the impression of doubling its height. At its peak, the tower's structure and cladding create a similar effect: engineered in a weave-like pattern, the skin becomes thinner and more transparent as the structural loads decrease higher up the tower. The pattern is inspired by a denglong, the traditional Chinese lantern made from woven bamboo strips. In the daytime, the tower will seem to fade into the sky as it rises and thins. At night, the tower will appear brighter as it rises, so that in foggy weather the light will seem to shine out of the clouds from an unknown source.

The design of the Guangzhou tower can be read as a simple picture of what distinguishes this city from others: the three rivers that form the foundation for a rising spirit of innovation. Seen from different locations around the city, the three curving towers will appear to change form and arrangement, creating unique silhouettes. From a distance they coalesce into a single object; from closer the weave of the three is visible; and from within, rising up in the elevator, the void itself dominates—a single, continuous, twisting volume containing within it the dynamic aspirations of the city. The tower becomes a dynamic presence on the skyline, a true landmark.

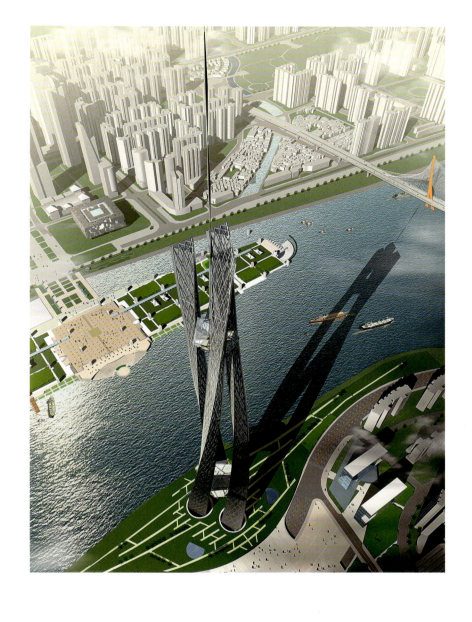

< ∧ The tower's geometry is a continuous transition of an equilateral triangle along a vertical axis, tapering as it rotates upward.

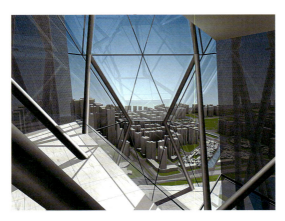

< Observation platform.

> View to building from the Pearl River.

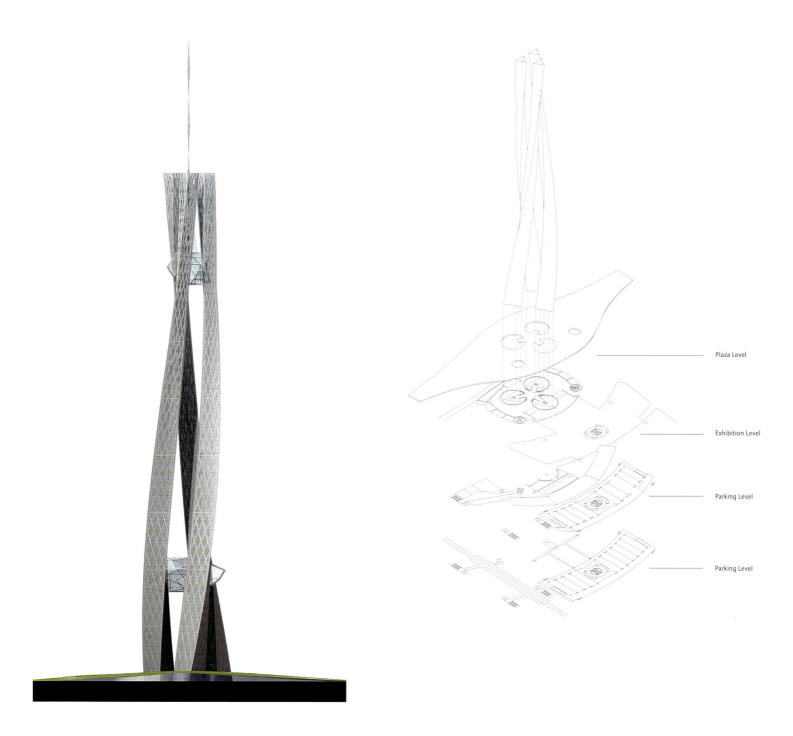

Plaza Level

Exhibition Level

Parking Level

Parking Level

SELECTED PROJECTS 1988 - 2005

1988 - 89
DWP Van Nuys Distribution Headquarters, Parking Structure
Van Nuys, CA
Ellerbe Becket

1991 - 92
DWP Central Distribution Headquarters Administration Building and Warehouse
Los Angeles, CA
Ellerbe Becket

1989 - 91
DWP Van Nuys Distribution Headquarters, Administration Building and Warehouse
Van Nuys, CA
Ellerbe Becket

1991 - 95
Los Angeles Metro Red Line Station at Vermont Avenue and Santa Monica Boulevard
Los Angeles, CA
Ellerbe Becket

1990
Overland Avenue House/Studio
Los Angeles, CA

1991
R.T.D. Corporate Headquarters
Los Angeles, CA
Ellerbe Becket

1990
West Coast Gateway Competition
Los Angeles, CA

1991 - 93
DWP Central Distribution Headquarters Fleet Services Facility
Los Angeles, CA
Ellerbe Becket

1991
Oxnard House
Oxnard, CA

1993
Sony 2000 Urban Entertainment Center Prototype
Los Angeles, CA
Ellerbe Becket

1993 - 94
Showscan CineMania Theater, Universal CityWalk
Universal City, CA
Ellerbe Becket

1993
Kemayoran Master Plan
Jakarta, Indonesia
Ellerbe Becket

1993
Yunsai Medical Tower Competition
Seoul, Korea
Ellerbe Becket

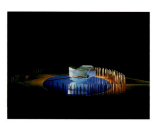

1993
Imax Theater
Oman
Ellerbe Becket

1993
Dubai Shooting Range & Academy
Dubai, United Arab Emirates
Ellerbe Becket

1994 - 97
Sinai Temple Akiba Academy Expansion
Los Angeles, CA
Dworsky Associates

1993
Telecommunications Tower
Jakarta, Indonesia
Ellerbe Becket

1996 - 98
El Sereno Pool and Recreation Center
Los Angeles, CA
Dworsky Associates

1993 - 95
West Hollywood City Hall Renovation
West Hollywood, CA
Ellerbe Becket

1996
Sweeney/Rubin Alumni and Visitor Center, University of California
Riverside, CA
Dworsky Associates

1997
Xinyizhuang Urban Redevelopment
Jinan, China
Dworsky Associates

1996 - 99
Lloyd D. George United States Courthouse
Las Vegas, NV
Dworsky Associates

1997 - 98
Beckman Hall Business and Technology Center, Chapman University
Orange, CA
Dworsky Associates

1998
Songdong Civic Center Design Competition
Seoul, Korea
Dworsky Associates

1997 - 99
Los Angeles Metro Red Line Extension at Cesar Chavez Boulevard and Soto Street
Los Angeles, CA
Dworsky Associates

1998
Korean Industrial Design Center Design Competition
Seoul, Korea
Dworsky Associates

1998
Korean Office Building Design Competition
Seoul, Korea
Dworsky Associates

2000
Los Angeles United States Courthouse Design Competition
Los Angeles, CA
Cannon Design

1998
Oakland Raiders Hall of Fame Design Competition
Oakland, CA
Dworsky Associates

2000
San Ramon Civic Center Design Competition
San Ramon, CA
Cannon Design

2002
Simon Wiesenthal Headquarters
Los Angeles, CA
Dworsky Associates

2002
**Tomihiro Museum of Shi-Ga
Design Competition**
Shi-Ga, Japan
Yazdani Studio of Cannon Design

2002
**The Royal Theater Playhouse
Design Competition**
Copenhagen, Denmark
Yazdani Studio of Cannon Design

2003
**Duxton Plain Public Housing
Design Competition**
Singapore
Yazdani Studio of Cannon Design

2003
Motorcycle Hall of Fame
Columbus, OH
Yazdani Studio of Cannon Design

2001
Cannon Design Offices
Los Angeles, CA
Cannon Design

1996 - 03
City of Santa Monica Public Safety Facility
Santa Monica, CA
Cannon Design

2000 - 03
Clark County Detention Center Expansion
Las Vegas, NV
Cannon Design

2001 - 04
**Yeshiva University of Los Angeles
Boys High School**
Los Angeles, CA
Videriksen Associates, Executive Architects

2000 - 04
Glendale Police Headquarters
Glendale, CA
Cannon Design

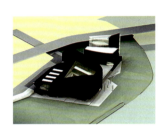

2002
Queensland Gallery of Modern Art Design Competition
Brisbane, Australia
Yazdani Studio of Cannon Design

2003
Korean Police Academy Design Competition
Seoul, Korea
Cannon Design

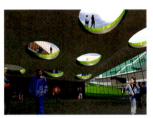

2002
Perth Amboy School Competition
Perth Amboy, NJ
Cannon Design

2003
Mary's Guest House
Austin, TX

2002 - 04
Student Services Building and Centralized Dining Facility, University of California
Berkeley, CA
Cannon Design

2003
Heatley Residence
Maui, HI

2002 - 04
Beverly Hills Public Works Headquarters and Water Treatment Facility
Beverly Hills, CA
Cannon Design

2002 - 04
Acosta Athletic Training Facility, University of California, Los Angeles
Los Angeles, CA
Cannon Design

2003
Contra Costa County Sheriff's Command Center
Martinez, CA
Yazdani Studio of Cannon Design

2003
Museum of Art and Design Competition, San Jose State University
San Jose, CA
Yazdani Studio of Cannon Design

2002 - 05
**Intercollegiate Athletics Building,
University of California**
Santa Barbara, CA
Cannon Design

2003 - 06
**Loker Student Union
California State University**
Dominguez Hills, CA
Cannon Design

2003 - 06
Long Beach GTE Middle School
Long Beach, CA
Cannon Design

2004
**Guangzhou TV and Sightseeing Tower
Design Competition**
Guangzhou, China
Yazdani Studio of Cannon Design

2004
Euro Inn
Prototype
Yazdani Studio of Cannon Design

2004
Alaska State Capitol Design Competition
Juneau, AK
Yazdani Studio of Cannon Design

2003 - 05
**Hauptman-Woodward Institute
Center for Structural Biology**
Buffalo, NY
Yazdani Studio of Cannon Design

2004 - 08
**Price Center Student Union Expansion,
University of California**
San Diego, CA
Yazdani Studio of Cannon Design

2005 - 08
**Science Building,
California State University**
Northridge, CA
Cannon Design

2005 - 08
**Cardiac Imaging Research Facility
Cedars-Sinai Medical Center**
Los Angeles, CA
Yazdani Studio of Cannon Design

RECOGNITION

Awards and Honors

Honor Award, 2005
American Institute of Architects, San Diego Chapter
Price Center Expansion, University of California, San Diego

American Architecture Award, 2005
The Chicago Athenaeum
Price Center Expansion, University of California, San Diego

American Architecture Award, 2005
The Chicago Athenaeum
Guangzhou TV and Sightseeing Tower Competition

Sustainable Design Award, 2005
Los Angeles Business Council
Santa Monica Public Safety Facility

Honor Award, 2004
Concrete Masonry Association of California and Nevada
Clark County Detention Center

Next LA Award, 2004
American Institute of Architects, Los Angeles Chapter
Guangzhou TV and Sightseeing Tower Competition

Merit Award, 2004
American Institute of Architects, California Council
Clark County Detention Center

American Architecture Award, 2004
Chicago Athenaeum
Duxton Plain Housing Competition

Citation for Design Excellence, 2003
AIA Justice Facility Design
Lloyd D. George U.S. Federal Building and Courthouse

Next LA Award, 2002
American Institute of Architects, Los Angeles Chapter
Tomihiro Museum of Shi-Ga, Japan

Merit Award, 2001
American Institute of Architects, California Council
Lloyd D. George U.S. Federal Building and Courthouse

Honor Award, 2001
American Institute of Architects, Nevada Chapter
Lloyd D. George U.S. Federal Building and Courthouse

Honor Award, 2001
American Institute of Architects, California Council
Los Angeles Metro Red Line Station

Merit Award, 2001
American Institute of Architects, Los Angeles Chapter
Los Angeles Metro Red Line Station

Honor Award, 2000
General Services Administration
Lloyd D. George U.S. Federal Building and Courthouse

American Architecture Award, 2000
The Chicago Athenaeum
Los Angeles Metro Red Line Station

Honor Award, 2000
American Institute of Architects, California Council
El Sereno Pool & Recreation Center

Merit Award, 2000
U.S. Department of Transportation
Los Angeles Metro Red Line Station

Citation, 1999
Los Angeles Chapter AIA
El Sereno Pool & Recreation Center

Urban Beautification Award, 1999
Los Angeles Business Council
Sinai Temple Akiba Academy Expansion

Urban Beautification Award, 1999
Los Angeles Business Council
El Sereno Pool & Recreation Center

Honor Award, 1998
American Institute of Architects, Nevada Chapter
Clark County Detention Center

Honor Award, 1998
American Institute of Architects, California Council
DWP Fleet Services Building

Merit Award, 1997
American Institute of Architects, Los Angeles Chapter
DWP Fleet Services Building

Award for Design Excellence, 1997
LA Cultural Affairs Commission
El Sereno Pool & Recreation Center

Honor Award, 1994
American Institute of Architects, California Council
CineMania Showscan Theater

Merit Award, 1993
American Institute of Architects, Los Angeles Chapter
DWP Van Nuys Distribution Headquarters

P/A Design Award, 1992
Progessive Architecture Magazine
Los Angeles Metro Red Line Station

Honor Award, 1992
American Institute of Architects, Los Angeles Chapter
DWP Central Distribution Headquarters

Award for Design Excellence, 1992
LA Cultural Affairs Commission
DWP Fleet Service Building

Honor Award, 1992
Concrete Masonry Association of California and Nevada
DWP Central Distribution Headquarters

Selected Exhibitions

"LA 34," A+D Museum, Los Angeles, 2004

"Jewish Identity in Architecture," Jewish History Museum, Amsterdam, 2004 - 06

"Emerging Voices," New York, NY, 2003

"A New World Trade Center," Max Protetch Gallery, New York, NY, 2001

"New Blood 101," Los Angeles, CA/New York, NY, 2000

Light Construction Exhibit, Museum of Modern Art, New York, NY, 1995

Selected Publications

Buckham, Tom and Fred O. Williams: "Building's Design and Purpose Embody Hope for City's Revival," The Buffalo News, May 12, 2005
Newman, Morris: "Designing for Secure Buildings," LA Architect, June 2004
Sommer, Mark: "Building on Talent," Hauptman-Woodward Medical Research Institute, The Buffalo News, May 4, 2003
Milionis, Allison: "Drawing the Line; Sketchbooks of Mehrdad Yazdani," LA Architect, November/December 2002
Protetch, Max: A New World Trade Center: Design Proposals from Leading Architects Worldwide, New York, Regan Books, 2002
"A Fancy New Spot in Vegas," The New York Times, Summer 2001
Milshtein, Amy: "Judging Vegas," Contract, August 2001
"The GSA on Trial," Architecture, January 2001
Riddle, Danette: "Profile: Mehrdad Yazdani," LA Architect, September/October 2000
"News: Federal Building and United States Courthouse, Las Vegas, Nevada," Architecture, April 2000
Metro Red Line Vermont/Santa Monica Station, World Architecture, April 2000
"Red Lining" Metro Red Line Vermont/Santa Monica Station, Interior Design, April 2000
"Welcome Sight," Federal Building and United States Courthouse, Las Vegas, Nevada, Las Vegas Sun, Metro Section, May 8, 2000
Dean, Andrea Oppenheimer: "Down Under... in L.A.?" Metro Red Line Vermont/Santa Monica Station, Contract, March 2000
"The Nation's Biggest Landlord Just Found Style," Architectural Record, February 2000 (Lloyd D. George Federal Building and U.S. Courthouse)
Barreneche, Raul: "Rolling Out the Red Line," Travel & Leisure, November 1999
Giovannini, Joseph: Portfolio, Architecture, September 1999
Hay, David: "In Los Angeles, Set-Dressing the Subway," The New York Times Sunday Edition, Art/Architecture Section, December 20, 1998
"Flashy Art, Flashy Town," The Los Angeles Times, July 8, 1998
"25 of L.A.'s Most Well-Regarded Architects," The Los Angeles Business Journal, June 22, 1998
Giovannini, Joseph: "Showcase for Emerging Voices of California Modern," The New York Times, April 1998
"Showscan Cinemania" (Cover), AW Architektur & Wettbewerbe, March 1998
"Songdong Civic Center Complex," Architecture, October 1997
"Los Angeles Department of Water & Power, Fleet Services Building and Showscan CineMania Theater," A + U, June 1997
"Computers, Holdouts to Converts - Federal Building and United States Courthouse, Las Vegas," Architecture, February 1997
Newman, Morris: "Power Complex-Los Angeles Department of Water and Power Fleet Service Building" Architecture, July 1996
"New Civic Buildings: Federal Building and United States Courthouse, Las Vegas," Architecture, April 1996
"Federal Architecture: A New Era-Federal Building and United States Courthouse, Las Vegas," Architecture, January 1996
581 Architects in the World, Gallery Ma, Tokyo, Japan, 1995
International Architecture Yearbook, Images Australia Pty Ltd, 1995 (Showscan Cinemania)
"The Power of Architecture," Architectural Design, March 1995
Philip-A Guide to Recent Architecture Los Angeles, Philip-Puhverman, Hrtemi's, London, Zurich, Munich, 1995
"Filtration Plant," Architectural Design, February 1995
"New Visions for Old Age-Continuing Care Community," Architecture, October 1994
Hoyt, Charles K.: "Virtually Thrilling," Architectural Record, August 1994 (Showscan Cinemania)
"Vermont/Santa Monica Metro Red Line Station," World Cities Los Angeles, June 1994
"Vermont/Santa Monica Metro Red Line Station," Architectural Design, June 1994
"New City Hall in West Hollywood," LA Architect, April 1994
"A Shooting Range in Dubai," l'ARCA, November 1993
Whiteson, Leon: "Municipal Design Revolution - Gritty Elegance," The Los Angeles Times, July 1993
RTD Headquarters in L.A., l'ARCA, June 1993
Vermont/Santa Monica Station, l'ARCA, May 1993
Sheine, Judith: "Beyond Utility," Architecture, February 1993 (Los Angeles Department of Water and Power)
"39th Annual P/A Awards," Progressive Architecture, January 1992

ACKNOWLEDGMENTS

This volume reflects two decades of collaboration and represents the talents of many people. I would like to extend my deepest appreciation to each of those individuals whose dedicated efforts have contributed to the work in this book.

In particular, I would like to acknowledge the following for their vision, inspiration, and support: Craig Booth, James Braam, John Chan, Katherine Decker, Doug Dworsky, John Frane, Max Frixione, Bung Ko, Yan Krymsky, Carlos Madrid, Hadrian Predock, Philip Ra, Andrew Wong, and Jessica Yi.

For their mentorship and influence in helping me to navigate my career, I am indebted to Michael Graves, Louis M. Naidorf, Daniel Dworsky, and Mark Mendell.

I am grateful to my partners and colleagues at Cannon Design for their support of this publication. I owe special thanks to Lesley Grant, Alexandra Schioldager, and Cynthia Hilliers, who have carried this book from concept to completion, to Joseph Giovannini for his eloquent introduction, and to John Tom and Andrew Blum for their tremendous dedication. Also I would like to thank Ann Gray and Jesse Brink at Balcony Press, and Peter Shamray at Navigator Cross-media.

I wish to dedicate this book to my parents, Bahram and Mahrokh Yazdani, and to my wife Hoda and daughter Jeyraan.

Project Credits

Rember Aleman
Ira Amanowicz
Dana Barbera
Jose Barez
Audrey Barrett
Hernan Bejarano
Ron Benson
Chip Berry
Brit Billeaud
Craig Booth
James Braam
Samuel Burnett
Paciencia Castelo
John Chan
Ignatius Chau
Lily Chiu
Benjamin Cien
George Cranston
Ed Crayne
Radames Culqui
Marc Davidson
Paul Davis
Katherine Decker
Katherine Demetriou
Vicki Desch
Art Dungo
Daniel Dworsky
Douglas Dworsky
Steve Fader
Rue Fort
John Frane
Max Frixione
Gary Friar
Tom Goffigon
Robert Griffith
Alireza Hadian
Cici Han
Craig Hamilton
Heidi Hefferlin
Holly Helin
Judi Hodge
Alicja Hrabia
Fred Javier
Kenneth Killian
Bung Ko
Su-Jin Ko
Yan Krymsky
Marion LaRue
Sing Sing Lee
Jim LeFever
Robert Levine
Greg Lombardi
David Macleod
Carlos Madrid
James Matson
Russell McCarley
Allison Milionis
Gary Miller
Rudolfo Modina
Claudia Morello
Alan Morishige
Karen Munson
Louis Naidorf
Pedro Newburn
Robert Newsom
Marios Nimitz
Eddie Nishi
Craig Norman
Joseph O'Neil
Chris Ossa
Hansol Park
Simon Park
Debbie Pearson
Sara Pelone
Juan Perez
Jack Poulin
Vernon Pounds
Hadrian Predock
Anne Laurie Prichard
Jon Pugh
Philip Ra
Matt Ralsten
Scott Reed
Danette Riddle
Gustavo Ripalda
Aaron Ritenour
Robert Rosenberg
Ken Rossi
Steven Ruef
Cielocita Sacilioc
Rey Sacilioc
Laurie Salmore
Luz Sanez
Alexandra Schioldager
Frank Sica
Karl Smith
Michael Smith
Rita Spring
Iris Steinbeck
Asli Suner
Juliet Taft
Sallyann Thomas
Michael Tunkey
Yassi Vafai
Teena Videriksen
Bruce Weinstein
Andrew Wong
David Woo
Jessica Yee
Terence Young
Tommy Yuen
Michele Zappen
Alek Zarifian

Photography Credits

Peter Aaron/Esto Photography, pp. 103-109

Farshid Assassi, pp. 54-57, 63, 66-69, 71-75, 113-117

Tom Bonner, pp. 24, 29-31, 32, 37-39, 70

Jeff Goldberg/ Esto Photography, pp. 40-43

Tim Griffith, pp. 49-53

Timothy Hursley, pp. 25-27, 33-35

John Edward Linden, pp. 49-53, 58-61

Adrian Vilicescu, pp. 16-23, 86-89

Presentation painting from "A New World Trade Center: Design Proposals," an exhibit at the Max Protetch Gallery in New York City, December, 2001, featuring proposals from some of the world's leading architects asked to envision how the 16-acre World Trade Center site in lower Manhattan might be re-developed.